WITH HONOR AND INTEGRITY

With Honor and Integrity

Transgender Troops in Their Own Words

Edited by

Máel Embser-Herbert *and* Bree Fram

NEW YORK UNIVERSITY PRESS

New York

NEW YORK UNIVERSITY PRESS
New York
www.nyupress.org

The views expressed in this publication are those of the authors and contributors and do not necessarily reflect the official policy or position of the Department of Defense or the U.S. Government.

References to Internet websites (URLs) were accurate at the time of writing. Neither the author nor New York University Press is responsible for URLs that may have expired or changed since the manuscript was prepared.

Library of Congress Cataloging-in-Publication Data
Names: Embser-Herbert, Máel, 1956–   editor. | Fram, Bree, editor.
Title: With honor and integrity : transgender troops in their own words /
edited by Máel Embser-Herbert, and Bree Fram.
Other titles: Transgender troops in their own words
Description: New York : NYU Press, [2021] | Series: LGBTQ politics series |
Includes bibliographical references and index.
Identifiers: LCCN 2021013292 | ISBN 9781479801039 (hardback) |
ISBN 9781479820474 (paperback) | ISBN 9781479801053 (ebook) |
ISBN 9781479801077 (ebook other)
Subjects: LCSH: Transgender military personnel—United States. | Transgender military
personnel—Government policy—United States.
Classification: LCC UB418.T72 W58 2021 | DDC 355.0092/670973—dc23
LC record available at https://lccn.loc.gov/2021013292

New York University Press books are printed on acid-free paper, and their binding materials are chosen for strength and durability. We strive to use environmentally responsible suppliers and materials to the greatest extent possible in publishing our books.

Manufactured in the United States of America

10 9 8 7 6 5 4 3 2

Also available as an ebook

CONTENTS

PREFACE

Entire volumes have been written—and debates continue—over what the word "transgender" means, who it includes, and what is appropriately viewed as transgender history. We can provide here only a brief introduction. We also offer a small window into military service and some military terms that may be unfamiliar. While we have attempted to include most explanations within the text, we also provide a glossary that you may find helpful.

GLAAD, formerly the Gay and Lesbian Alliance Against Defamation, defines transgender as:

> An umbrella term for people whose gender identity and/or gender expression differs from what is typically associated with the sex they were assigned at birth. People under the transgender umbrella may describe themselves using one or more of a wide variety of terms—including *transgender*. . . . Many transgender people are prescribed hormones by their doctors to bring their bodies into alignment with their gender identity. Some undergo surgery as well. But not all transgender people can or will take those steps, and a transgender identity is not dependent upon physical appearance or medical procedures.[1]

The vast majority of our contributors identify within a binary conception of gender, meaning that gender is imagined as limited to two categories, the feminine and the masculine. Some contributors may have nonbinary gender identities, identities that bridge the feminine and the masculine, or identities that vary across time. But because the military accepts only a binary construction of gender, one must present within that binary, regardless of how one might actually identify.

Another concept frequently discussed with regard to transgender people, and one that is especially salient to the accounts presented here, is transition. Generally, transition is how transgender people define and describe the steps they take to bring their external appearance into congruence with their internal identity. For many, the process of transition includes hormone replacement therapy (HRT), which modifies secondary sex characteristics and does a good deal of the work in altering appearance. Some transgender people pursue surgical procedures, while others may transition without such intervention. It is also important to note that a person may identify as transgender and, for a variety of reasons, never transition medically, legally, and/or socially.

Transgender people have been around for all of recorded human history and have been referred to by many names across cultures. Of course, this text cannot begin to explore transgender identities and culture beyond the issue on which we focus, military service. Given the attention paid to the fiftieth anniversary of Stonewall, you may be familiar with the names, if not the lives of, Marsha P. Johnson or Sylvia Rivera. But most transgender people in history do not appear in history books or the media. We encourage our readers to explore transgender people and identities throughout history and around the world, whether that be Lou Sullivan[2] or Lucy Hicks Anderson[3] in the United States or the hijras of South Asia and the *fa'afafine* of Polynesia.[4] Unfortunately, many transgender individuals and groups have been erased from the historical record, often by the very communities in which they lived as well as by conquerors and colonizers. Those conquering armies, knowingly or unknowingly, had transgender individuals serving in them, but the relevant historical record outside the last several hundred years is spotty and anecdotal at best. We address this briefly in the first chapter.

Transgender individuals serve in the military for many reasons, and we'll let our contributors speak for themselves, but for some people the draw is a unique military culture that varies by nation and by service branch. In the United States, the armed services are the Air Force, Army, Coast Guard, Marine Corps, and Navy—and, as of December 2019, the

Space Force. For some, the attraction of military service may be the camaraderie or shared sense of purpose that the military offers. For others, it may be more tangible desires such as job security, benefits, or travel. Regardless of what motivates one to join, military service requires a measure of self-sacrifice and a willingness to accept the culture of the military. Absent that commitment, an individual's years in service are likely to be fraught with internal and external conflict.

Each military service has identified core values from which everything else in its culture builds. These include, but are not limited to, commitment, devotion to duty, honor, integrity, loyalty, personal courage, respect, and selfless service. Resolving the conflict between an individual's values, the values of society at large, and the values a military service holds dear or professes to possess is a central theme of many of the stories you are about to read. For the transgender individuals in this book who had to conceal their identity for some or all of their time in service, consider how they had to balance the service's professed values of honor and integrity against who they were. Think about how much they were willing to value selfless service and devotion to duty over who they were as individuals.

We know that not every reader comes to this volume with an understanding of or support for transgender people and we know that not every reader comes to their reading with an understanding of or support for military service. In fact, we very much hope that to be the case. But we also hope that such readers will learn from these accounts. The essays presented here illuminate not only the lives of transgender military personnel, but of trans lives, generally, and of military members putting service before self. We hope you enjoy sharing the journey.

GLOSSARY

chiefs: a collective term for the Navy's three highest enlisted ranks

cis or cisgender: a person whose gender identity is consistent with their sex assigned at birth

commission: an appointment to serve as an officer in the military

cutter: Coast Guard term for any ship that has been commissioned, i.e., given a name and a full-time crew

DADT: "Don't Ask, Don't Tell" was a federal law implemented by Congress under President Clinton that was in effect from 1994 to 2011; it barred lesbians, gays, and bisexuals from serving openly, but attempted to limit the ability of the Department of Defense to investigate service members without direct evidence

DEERS: Defense Enrollment Eligibility Reporting System, the official database of personnel information within the Department of Defense

DoD: Department of Defense

E1–E9: enlisted pay grades

gender dysphoria: a diagnosis indicating psychological distress that results from incongruence between one's sex assigned at birth and one's gender identity; it should be noted that not all people who experience gender incongruence experience psychological distress

gender reassignment surgery (GRS): surgery to bring a person's body into alignment with their gender identity; also referred to as sex reassignment surgery (SRS) and gender confirmation surgery (GCS)

GI Bill: financial assistance for higher education

Individual Ready Reserve (IRR): members of the reserve forces that, though they may be, are not typically subject to being recalled to duty and are not attached to a unit

real-life experience (RLE): time during which one presents themselves to the world in accordance with their gender identity; some health care providers require it prior to certain surgeries or even hormone use, though this requirement is increasingly rare

(Ret.): retired

ROTC: Reserve Officers' Training Corps; organization that trains individuals who are attending civilian colleges and grants them a commission in one of the military services upon graduation

squadron coin: small medallion typically bearing an organization's insignia or emblem and representing significant accomplishments or membership in an organization

SEAL: Sea, Air, and Land Forces; U.S. Navy's primary special operations force

sex reassignment surgery (SRS): see gender reassignment surgery

SPARTA: Organization that advocates for actively serving transgender military members, veterans, and their families

TAVA: Transgender American Veterans Association; organization that advocates for the equality of transgender veterans and active duty service members

transitioning: process of changing one's gender presentation to be consistent with one's gender identity

transphobia: negative attitudes about and/or actions toward transgender people based on a range of emotions including, but not limited to, discomfort and fear

Introduction

Living our truths has made us all stronger and more devoted
to our duty, with no secrets to hide behind we can be fully
engaged.
—Hospital Corpsman Third Class Akira Wyatt

According to the United States Department of Defense (DoD), "The men and women serving in our armed forces have helped forge a sense of identity and unity among Americans, particularly during times of strife."[1] Yet, rather than forging a sense of "identity and unity among Americans," the military has become a pawn in a political battle, questioning identity, disrupting unity, and leading to, rather than minimizing, strife. The subject of debate is no longer the service of African Americans or women, or even of lesbians, gay men, and bisexuals. Rather, debate over the past few years has centered on the military service of transgender individuals. Many do not realize that "Don't Ask, Don't Tell," a federal law that prevented lesbian, gay, and bisexual personnel from serving openly, did not address the presence of transgender persons. Thus, despite its repeal in 2011, transgender military service remained prohibited.

It seems reasonably safe to assume that most Americans do not know, or do not know that they know, a transgender person who has served or is serving in our military, despite data from 2014 suggesting that 15,500 transgender persons serve in the military and 134,300 military veterans identify as transgender.[2] Yet humanizing those we do not know or understand is one avenue to, if not changing minds, furthering the conversation. This volume seeks to bring the experiences of transgender military personnel, past, present, and future, to a wide audience. In doing so, we illustrate that transgender military personnel have served

1

honorably and that, rather than being a detriment to military readiness, their presence is beneficial.

Though our focus is the more recent service of transgender military personnel, what we offer as a more contemporary account would be incomplete if we failed to first acknowledge those who have, in centuries past, served with the military by appearing to be someone of a different gender. Typically, because of gendered restrictions on military service, it was women who presented themselves as men. For some, this decision was based on a desire to follow male partners into service; for others, it was a desire to engage in work, whether for livelihood or patriotism, from which women were barred. Rupert Neville, writing in the *Salt Lake Tribune* in July 1910, observed, "More often, women have adopted man's attire through sheer love of adventure and a dislike of the limitations and restraints imposed on their own sex."[3] While these individuals may or may not have identified as what we would today view as transgender, their experiences serve as an important backdrop to the current discussions regarding transgender military service. In short, presenting as a sex/gender different from that assigned at birth—including while serving in the military—while a relatively new matter of debate, is not a new phenomenon.

Unlike some of the debates about the gender identity of historical figures, today's controversy does not revolve around the authenticity of a gender presentation that differs from that assigned at birth. Rather, debates about the ability of transgender people to serve in the military seem to center on arguments about whether they can do so without their presence negatively impacting the military. It seems, then, that the relevant question is not whether those who, in the past, served in a sex/gender other than that assigned at birth identified as transgender—as we use and understand the term today—but rather whether their presence was disruptive or not. Their motivation, and whether their gender presentation was temporary, is irrelevant. If we know that, in the 19th century, at least some of those assigned female at birth were—even when that status was revealed—recognized as having made valuable and honorable contributions to the nation through their service, why is this even an issue in the 21st century?

Many stories of women serving as men come from around the globe and predate the U.S. Civil War, the most frequently discussed period with regard to cross-gender service in the United States. Some lived as men only while performing military service. Others served as men and lived as men for the remainder of their lives. In France, for example, Chevalier d'Éon (1728–1810) was identified as female-bodied only many years after military service, upon death.[4] In 1815, William Brown joined the Royal Navy, soon to be discharged for "being a female."[5] According to the National Archives of the United Kingdom, "It was not unheard of in the 18th and 19th centuries for women to disguise themselves as men and join the Royal Navy—and some even managed to serve in this way for many years."[6]

The American Battlefield Trust states, "There are over 400 documented cases of women disguising themselves as men and fighting as soldiers on both sides during the Civil War."[7] In their comprehensive book, *They Fought Like Demons: Women Soldiers in the Civil War*, DeAnne Blanton and Lauren M. Cook provide detailed accounts of many who, while assigned female at birth, served in both the Union and Confederate armies as men. Albert Cashier served a full three-year enlistment with the 95th Illinois Infantry, mustering out on August 27, 1865. No one discovered that Cashier had been assigned female at birth until 1911, when he was injured and the doctor discovered that Cashier was female-bodied. He lived as a man until death, suggesting to some that, as opposed to seeking only the daring life of a soldier, Cashier did, in fact, identify as a man. Blanton and Cook describe Cashier's challenges with physical and mental health and the way "former comrades in the 95th Illinois Infantry rallied around Cashier," writing, "[Cashier] was one of them, after all, and [his] sex did not change their attitude."[8]

An extensive article titled "Females Posed as Men" appeared in the *St. Paul Globe* on February 3, 1901. The author describes a number of cases where women presented themselves as men. In several instances, these are accounts of civilian lives. For example, the author writes, "For forty-two years Louis Herman has been traveling around the world as a man. She goes as a courier, speaks several languages, and behaves like a man of the world."[9] This case illustrates that, without question, some who were assigned female at birth sought to live as men throughout their lives, not just for the sake of military service. The article ends with the mention of Otto Schaffer, who "lived a hermit's life in Kansas for many years, after having fought in several battles. Although Schaffer was found after death to be a woman, [Schaffer] was given a soldier's funeral."[10] According to Blanton and Cook, Schaffer's funeral was provided by his comrades of the local Grand Army Veterans post.

Accounts such as these suggest that what was most important was whether or not an individual was viewed as having performed their service well. In their conclusion regarding those assigned female at birth who served in the U.S. Civil War while presenting as men, Blanton and Cook write:

> Taken as a group, women were successful soldiers. If their aim was the same as the majority of the three million men who enlisted—to contribute to the war effort to the best of their ability—then women soldiers accomplished their goal. . . . With gender prejudices and stereotyping removed from consideration of their performance as soldiers, women were given and accomplished the same assignments in camp and on the battlefield. . . . [W]omen who heeded the call to defend their country were overwhelmingly effective in their martial roles.[11]

Some are no doubt familiar with Christine Jorgensen, who served in World War II and, after leaving military service, later traveled to Denmark for transition-related surgery. Fewer realize that Jorgensen was not the only former service member to do so. For example, Charlotte McLeod and Tamara Edel Rees also transitioned after leaving military service. McLeod, who served in the Army in the late 1940s, was the second U.S. woman to travel to Denmark for surgery. Rees, a former paratrooper, obtained surgery in the Netherlands. Their stories show us that people who understood their authentic sex/gender to be other than that assigned at birth, regardless of when they transitioned, have participated in the military across time, and certainly in the modern military. Doubtless many more remain unidentified.

A more recent and somewhat puzzling story is that of Sergeant Joanna Clark, later Sister Mary Elizabeth. Assigned male at birth, Clark enlisted in the Navy in 1957, eventually becoming a chief petty officer. After serving about twelve years and upon realizing that she was transgender, Clark was honorably discharged and, in 1975, underwent what was then referred to as sex reassignment surgery. In 1976, Clark appeared at the Army Reserve Center in Los Alamitos, California, seeking to reenlist and not hiding the fact that she was transgender. "Lt. Col. Art Wolford, U.S. Army (ret.), an administrator for the 49th Medical Battalion, assured her the sex-change operation didn't matter."[12] Wolford said in an interview, "I'm the one who enlisted her, and she made absolutely no attempt to hide her background. . . . It doesn't bother me one bit. She was a person qualified to do the job we needed done."[13] The Department of the Army felt differently and nineteen months after enlisting Clark was again discharged. Sounding an awful lot like the rhetoric of today in citing a "change of sex" as grounds for disqualification, a statement on behalf of the Army read, "It is the Department of the Army policy not to waive this disqualification due to the requirement for continuing maintenance therapy and the high incidence of psychological problems associated with the condition."[14] Clark brought suit against the Army, receiving a settlement of $25,000 and an honorable discharge.[15]

In 1992, attorney and trans activist Phyllis Randolph Frye created and hosted the First International Conference on Transgender Law and Employment Policy. Held in Houston, Texas, the conference addressed trans people's legal rights regarding a range of issues including criminal justice, employment, health care, housing, marriage, and military service. At this conference, attorney Sharon Stuart, who had served in the U.S. Marine Corps as an attorney during the Vietnam era, presented on military law. She began by discussing the way that a prohibition on cross-dressing was used to target gender-transgressive military personnel, stating that "there have been instances in which the military confused homosexuality and cross dressing and tried to discharge personnel as homosexuals when indeed they were not."[16] This is important for its illustration of both the conflation of sexual orientation and gender identity and the degree to which the military was ill-equipped to deal with these issues. It is also important for the fact that these conversations were taking place almost thirty years ago.

At the second conference, in 1993, Stuart described her work with the Military Law Project, highlighting a revised mission statement that included the paragraph:

> To provide consultation and information to transgendered [sic] military personnel confronted with disciplinary and administrative actions by the military and to inform their military and civilian legal counsel regarding gender related issues; to draft and distribute legal do's and don'ts for transgendered [sic] military personnel; to inform them of their legal rights and obligation as service members.[17]

It was also noted that "[d]uring 1992 and the early part of '93, the Military Law Project made contact with eighteen people who were confronted with administrative action, medical discharge and other legal problems related to cross gender behavior in the military."[18] At that conference, the Military Law Project and Survey, a pilot study regarding transgender military service, was launched. The goal was to obtain 250 completed questionnaires and share them with the Department of Defense.

After the conference, work on the Military Survey Questionnaire, as it was then called, continued. The survey was, at twenty-two pages, quite lengthy and expensive to print and distribute. Potentially even more impactful on the response rate was the difficulty of locating participants. Much like the challenges faced by those organizations working with transgender military personnel today, the need to protect identities slowed the dissemination of information. In a 1994 report, Stuart indicated that they had received about fifty completed questionnaires.[19] While the success of additional data collection is unclear, archival materials leave little doubt that transgender people were serving in the U.S. military and sought to remain in service. Despite the fact that many in the general public were unaware of the issue until 2016, it is clear that, regardless of whether they would have used the term "transgender" or not, gender-variant people have always served in the military.

Signed into law in 1993, "Don't Ask, Don't Tell" (DADT)[20] addressed only cisgender lesbian, gay, and bisexual people, not those who identified as transgender. Thus, when it was repealed, DoD policy continued to bar trans people from serving openly. Then, on June 30, 2016, Secretary of Defense Ash Carter announced a DoD policy that officially lifted the ban on transgender military service. As a result, current members of the armed forces as well as veterans began to come out publicly and seek gender-affirming care and resources. This period of acceptance lasted for a brief thirteen months until, on July 26, 2017, the newly elected President Trump posted a series of tweets in which he made clear that transgender individuals would yet again be barred from serving openly in the U.S. military. The rapid shift in policy created much confusion and anxiety, especially for those current service members whose livelihoods were now at risk. However, it is difficult to understand the complexities and nuances of the current situation without first understanding the military's long and complex history regarding sexuality, and sexual orientation in particular.

Until the 20th century, nonprocreative sex—specifically, sodomy—was criminalized as a sin against both God and society and viewed as an evil to which anyone might succumb. The military preferred to deal with it swiftly, punishing anyone who was caught, or even suspected of, having engaged in the prohibited behavior. In the 20th century, with the advent of psychiatry as a legitimate field of study, this outlook began to change. Psychiatrists began using new models of sexuality to understand their patients and classified sodomy as a mental defect associated primarily with a specific group of people—homosexuals. Within the context of the U.S. military, revisions to the Articles of War in 1917 and 1920 made both nonconsensual and consensual sodomy a military crime. By combining the new psychiatric ideologies with the codified criminalization of same-sex intimacy, a new "sodomist" category began to emerge in society, a box in which people who failed to conform to sex stereotypes could be placed. Between the two world wars, this homophobic bigotry slowly became institutionalized within U.S. military policy.

These practices led to two common but ill-informed beliefs that determined military policy from then on: (1) that gay[21] people were a distinct and dangerous identity, and (2) that stereotypical characteristics regarding gender were an accurate way to judge someone's sexuality. It became common practice to equate nonconformity with a personality disorder and the emphasis on the physical aspects of same-sex attraction led to the hypersexualization of gay people, especially cisgender gay men, as sexual deviants and predators. Additionally, systematic exclusion based on stereotypes precipitated the practice of defining a person as homosexual even if there was no sex act for which one could be found guilty. It was no longer homosexual acts that were being criminalized; it was the very status of homosexuality that was considered incompatible with military service. By the end of World War II, all gay people had been deemed unfit for service.

Following World War II, U.S. society experienced a surge of "traditional" values—commitment to morality, family, and religion among them—which led to two major events, the Lavender Scare and the growth of the religious right. The Lavender Scare took place in the 1950s concurrent with Senator Joseph McCarthy's anticommunist Red Scare. Like the Red Scare, the Lavender Scare incited moral panic in the American people; while the Red Scare focused on uncovering Communists, this panic stemmed from the fear that gay people had "infiltrated" the American government. These Red and Lavender scares, and subsequent conservative panics, led to the rise of the New Christian Right as a politically active force. They pushed for a strong military and traditional values, focusing on limiting reproductive rights and later on same-sex marriage. As this new political force grew in influence, its members increasingly became involved in the military itself, especially in high-ranking offices. With regard to the military, far-right evangelicals joined the military in the hopes of achieving positions of power and authority. Between the earlier codification of antigay policies in the military and the now large amount of political power held by the New Christian Right, the political maneuvering regarding DADT was almost inevitable.

The controversy surrounding the creation and implementation of what would eventually come to be known as DADT had begun in 1991 when Bill Clinton, during his presidential campaign, pledged to lift the ban on the open military service of lesbians, gays, and bisexuals. At the time Clinton made his pledge, the policy in place was Department of Defense Directive 1332.14, implemented in January 1982 as a result of two cases that served to highlight the arbitrary and capricious way the system treated gay service members. Ensign Vernon E. (Copy) Berg III and Air Force Technical Sergeant Leonard Matlovich were two successful and competent service members who had received "other than honorable" discharges in January and October 1975, respectively. However, prior to the 1982 directive, military regulations contained a loophole that allowed service members with distinguished service histories to be retained despite an accusation of homosexuality. Both men achieved a critical victory when the District of Columbia Court of Appeals ruled in their favor, relying on that very loophole. The D.C. Court of Appeals found that neither the Navy nor the Air Force produced sufficient evidence as to why Berg and Matlovich could not be retained due to their impressive records thus far and sent inquiries to the respective branches asking for an explanation. When, over the next two years, neither branch offered an explanation, the D.C. Court of Appeals ordered Berg and Matlovich to be reinstated. Although the men ultimately took cash settlements from the military in exchange for resigning and not appealing the case to the U.S. Supreme Court, the case revealed the hypocrisy of a system that led to the creation of the new DoD directive, closing the loophole and making clear that the military service of those who were openly lesbian, gay, or bisexual was unacceptable. It declared:

> Homosexuality is incompatible with military service. The presence in the military environment of persons who engage in homosexual conduct or who, by their statements, demonstrate a propensity to engage in homosexual conduct, seriously impairs the accomplishment of the military mission. The presence of such members adversely affects the ability of the Military Services to maintain discipline, good order, and morale; to foster mutual trust and confidence among service members, to ensure the integrity of the system of rank and command; to facilitate assignment and worldwide deployment of service members who frequently must live and work under close conditions affording minimal privacy; to recruit and retain members of the Military Services; to maintain the public acceptability of military service; and to prevent breaches of security.[22]

In addition to the new directive, top military officials, such as the chair of the Joint Chiefs of Staff, General Colin Powell, expressed hostility toward any political step, executive order or otherwise, that would move the military closer to tolerating openly gay military service. Thus, when Clinton made the pledge to end the ban, he unleashed a fierce debate that would follow him through the rest of his campaign and most of his presidency.

On January 21, 1993, the day after his inauguration, President Clinton agreed to a six-month delay on lifting the ban, citing the need for a study period during which the DoD could contribute to the creation of a new policy. Certain measures, though, were implemented immediately, namely, the removal of questions asking recruits about their sexual orientation and the halt of discharges on the basis of sexual orientation. Those found to be lesbian, gay, or bisexual during this study period would instead be placed in an inactive, unpaid, reserve status until a decision could be made regarding a new policy. Following the announcement of the delay, on January 25, President Clinton held a meeting with

the Joint Chiefs of Staff reiterating his commitment to ending discrimination in the military, though the "group told the president that such a
move would 'seriously undermine morale and discipline, disrupt military readiness and threaten recruiting.'"[23] Undeterred, four days later, on
January 29, President Clinton instructed Secretary of Defense Les Aspin
to prepare an executive order ending discrimination in the military on
the basis of sexual orientation. It was to be signed on July 15, at the completion of the six-month study period. On February 4, 1993, two weeks
and one day after President Clinton's inauguration, the Republican Research Committee's Task Force on Military Personnel began hearings in
the House of Representatives on the issue of ending the ban on the open
military service of lesbian, gay, and bisexual personnel.

The first House hearings were chaired by Representative Jon Kyl (R-
AZ) and Representative Cliff Stearns (R-FL) and consisted primarily
of testimony by other representatives—a large number veterans themselves—as well as retired senior military officers. Overall, the hearing
was skewed to support a decision on which the committee members
had already come to an agreement: the ban on open service must not
be lifted in any way, shape, or form. As Nathaniel Frank, historian and
author of *Unfriendly Fire: How the Gay Ban Undermines the Military
and Weakens America*, states, the hearing and the study period itself
was simply an act of political savvy and the "time would not be used to
learn, but to let opposition fester and grow."[24] For instance, one of the
most well-known and patently bigoted statements of the hearings came
from Admiral Thomas Moorer (U.S. Navy, Ret.), who testified that the
issues of gays in the military was "the most disturbing that I've ever en-
countered in war or peace because what is going on here is an effort in
effect to downgrade and demean and break down the whole structure
of our military forces," adding, "I can guarantee you that these young
people . . . will spot a homosexual a mile away as soon as he comes in,
and they'll have to name him Tessie or Agnes, or whatever, and then
subsequently he'll get caught in some kind of sexual activity and then
he's discharged."[25]

Disregarding, for now, the seemingly impossible admission that somehow the most disturbing thing Admiral Moorer had seen in peace *and* war was the move to end hateful discrimination against a marginalized group, it remains shockingly evident that there was no real proof behind his beliefs. First, he relied on outdated and incorrect assumptions regarding the conflation of sexuality and gender identity: that one can "tell" someone's sexuality based on gender stereotypes and that incongruity with one's assigned gender at birth automatically implies an "abnormal" sexuality. Second, he treated the very idea of showing respect to a gay person, specifically a gay officer, as ridiculous. However, his support for this view was simply his belief that it's impossible to show respect to a gay officer, creating a vicious cycle of reasoning that casts gay people as both the problem that needs to be solved and the reason the problem cannot be solved. This cycle can be seen in the way he foisted blame upon the younger generation of service members, assuming they would all take up this mantle of bigotry and *have to* give their superior officer a derogatory name ("Tessie or Agnes, or whatever") in lieu of the respect an officer deserves. Finally, Moorer propagated the harmful and unfounded stereotype that gay men are hypersexual and promiscuous. He did so by asserting that the only plausible course of action for an openly gay officer would be for that officer to be "caught in some kind of sexual activity," leading to their inevitable discharge. Although not all testimony at the House hearings was as outright in its bigotry, such sentiments were nonetheless reflected in a large portion of the statements made before Congress.

The House held additional hearings in May, this time with the House Committee on Armed Services, chaired by Representative Ronald Dellums (D-CA), who, supportive of eliminating the ban, was committed to a fair hearing for both parties. The first day of testimony, with primary witnesses being retired military personnel, involved much of the same rhetoric as the earlier hearings. The second day, however, the House heard testimony from a broader range of individuals, including members of law enforcement and academics. While there was not a perfect divide in tes-

timony where every person affiliated with the military wanted to maintain the ban and every person not affiliated with the military wanted to
end the ban, attitudes did tend to split along those lines. Sociologists and
psychologists such as Dr. David Segal and Dr. Gregory Herek provided
testimony that contradicted much of what people like Admiral Moorer
had been saying. Segal stated that if "somebody has been serving in the
unit for a while, has proven himself as a soldier, and then comes out, his
sexual orientation essentially becomes irrelevant."[26] Likewise, Herek believed that "neither group [heterosexuals or homosexuals] was inherently
incapable of adjusting to a policy under which gays and lesbians would
serve openly."[27] Thus, it remains important to note that, though the bigoted and incendiary language often received more attention, there was in
fact testimony that did advocate for a more relaxed stance on the military
service of lesbians, gay men, and bisexuals.

Following the House hearings, the debate went to the Senate, specifically, to the Committee on Armed Services. The hearings lasted from
mid-April into July and yielded much the same results as the House
hearings. On July 19, 1993, President Clinton announced what the new
policy regarding the open service of lesbians, gay men, and bisexuals would be, calling it an honorable compromise. After six months
of lengthy and rigorous debate, Public Law 103–160 passed both the
House and the Senate and, on November 30, 1993, was signed into law
by President Clinton. This policy would ultimately become known as
"Don't Ask, Don't Tell" (DADT). Despite being labeled a compromise,
the new law was nothing more than a mechanism for banning lesbians,
gay men, and bisexual persons from military service and, unlike earlier
prohibitions that had existed within branch regulations and could more
readily be changed, this prohibition was codified in federal law. And the
intended effect—halting the debate once and for all—failed. Instead, debate around the issue flourished for nearly another eighteen years, well
up until DADT's repeal took effect in 2011.

DADT had devastating consequences for both the individuals it
affected and the nation as a whole, but perhaps none as ironic as the

discharge of Arabic linguists. Between 1998 and 2003, i.e., the years immediately surrounding the terror attacks of September 11, 2001, the military had, under DADT, purged at least twenty-six Arabic and Farsi translators and linguists. The U.S. military had already been experiencing a shortage of Arabic translators largely due to the fact that Russian had been the military language of preference since the Cold War. Now the pool was shrinking further. This purge posed a real and present threat as the U.S. lost a great deal of its ability to collect data crucial to national security.

One way the government attempted to cope with this loss of talent was to contradict the very points that had been made regarding the presence of gay people in the military and their alleged negative impact on unit cohesion, morale, and readiness. The DoD gave authority to all military services to stop administrative discharges because it recognized the need for qualified soldiers, regardless of sexual orientation. That is, they permitted the military to retain the very people they had argued were damaging to the military. In doing so, DoD displayed how the ban (1) harmed American military efficiency and (2) caused the government and military officers to contradict themselves and their policies in an effort to maintain the personnel needed to fight in a situation such as the war in Iraq. Like Nathaniel Frank has said, this highlights the ways in which "prejudice is generally self-defeating rather than productive, and that it nearly always has unexpected consequences."[28]

In 2005, after a little over a decade of disparate implementation and enforcement, Representative Marty Meehan (D-MA) introduced the Military Readiness Enhancement Act. Had the legislation passed, it would have replaced DADT with a policy that prohibited discrimination on the basis of sexual orientation. However, the bill stalled in every committee in which it was introduced. Then, in 2008, Democratic lawmakers called for hearings to review DADT and begin the process of repealing the law. In a telling move, the Pentagon did not send a representative to defend DADT and other pro-ban supporters struggled to find credible witnesses. These hearings provided the foundation for the legislation Congress would pass two years later, the DADT Repeal Act of 2010, which took effect on September 20, 2011. Lesbian, gay, and bisexual service members could now serve openly alongside their heterosexual colleagues, as long as they all identified as cisgender. It marked a turning point of tolerance and acceptance in U.S. history. But it did not address the military service of transgender people.

* * *

Before we close this chapter, we would like to say something about the idea of gender itself. In September 1977, two sociologists, Candace West and Don H. Zimmerman, presented a conference paper in which they argued that people routinely "do gender" and that through our interactions with each other we are held accountable to a vast range of gendered norms and meanings.[29] In addition to these interactions, we are also held accountable by the organizations and institutions with which we coexist.[30] Ten years would pass before that work was published in the journal *Gender & Society* as "Doing Gender," an article viewed by many scholars as groundbreaking. West and Zimmerman described the purpose of the article as being "to advance a new understanding of gender as a routine accomplishment embedded in everyday interaction,"[31] employing theoretical reconceptualization rather than empirical research. Since that time, a robust body of empirical research has developed in the field, centered on the theory that, as opposed to simply "having" a gender, one "does" gender. Another ten years would pass before *Gender & Society* published an article centered on the transgender experience and even longer before anyone sought to use the concept of "doing gender" to explore it.[32]

The stories shared here complement this research on gender as an interactional accomplishment by illustrating, firsthand, how the lives of individuals embedded in an organization, in this case, the military, are very much structured by traditional conceptions of gender. For some, the only choice, if they wished to remain employed, was to suppress an authentic gender identity that conflicted with the one assigned at birth.

For others, a changing political landscape enabled them to pursue gender transition, some tentatively, others enthusiastically—and sometimes quite publicly. These accounts add to our understanding of the transgender experience, and the military experience in particular, by asking the reader to "hear" their authentic voices. We don't pretend that their voices are representative of the whole, but they are nonetheless important.

Though the sociological research on transgender lives is now flourishing, it was for years quite limited, with inquiry into the transgender military experience occurring only recently. Recent work explores transgender issues across a range of settings, highlighted by a number of excellent monographs. In *Trans Kids: Being Gendered in the Twenty-First Century*, Tey Meadow, a recipient of the American Sociological Association's Distinguished Scholarly Book Award for 2020, explores how families navigate the terrain of gender categorization and gender nonconformity. J. E. Sumerau and Lain Mathers, in *America through Transgender Eyes*, examine American society in a variety of settings, including religion and medicine. In *Unlivable Lives*, Laurel Westbrook interrogates violence and identity in the activism of trans rights organizations. Though few have explored the military, Cati Connell's forthcoming book on the changing policies of the military, including the repeal of "Don't Ask, Don't Tell," the integration of women into combat, and the ongoing battles over transgender inclusion, will no doubt be a welcome contribution to the literature.[33]

In February 2019, Andrew Grissom, senior associate librarian at Catalyst, Inc., compiled a bibliography of materials regarding transgender military service.[34] Grissom identified a limited number of books and films, most of which are auto/biographical and/or historical. In addition, Grissom provides citations for twenty-one articles. Although he describes this list as "selected," what he provides is representative of the limited body of work addressing transgender military service as an area of social scientific inquiry. Six of the articles focus on veterans, while one other is limited to the Canadian experience. Of the twenty-one articles, twelve centered on physical and/or mental health and twelve were published prior to 2016, when the policy of inclusion was announced. Of the eight articles published during or since 2016, only one does not center on health concerns and that paper is a case study of one individual, a retired military officer and civil servant who transitioned as a civilian in a military unit.[35] Further inquiry into the experiences of transgender military personnel is badly needed, not only to document an important period of national and institutional history, but as an additional contribution to the field of gender, both generally and with regard to the intersection of gender and organizations.

In a recent article, Embser-Herbert explored the experiences of transgender military personnel since 2016, when the Obama administration announced a policy of trans inclusion, which was followed, thirteen months later, by the Trump administration's announcement of a return to a policy of exclusion.[36] That work, based on a small sample of interviews, served as a starting point for further conversation regarding how transgender lives illuminate our understanding of gender. This volume, however, moves in another direction. Rather than position transgender military personnel as research subjects, this volume centers these individuals and their voices.

Embser-Herbert began by inviting one of their respondents, Bree Fram, to serve as a co-editor on the project. As co-editors, we then sought to identify individuals willing to submit personal essays regarding their experiences as transgender service members. Calls for participants were placed with SPARTA and TAVA, organizations for transgender military service members and veterans, respectively. We also relied on limited snowball "sampling" to identify potential participants. It felt important to include not only the voices of those currently serving, but also the stories of those who had realized they were trans, but who—if they wished to remain in the military—had been unable to come out due to earlier policies of exclusion. Since we knew that there were valuable stories from those who might not be comfortable offering their own writing, additional interviews were conducted. Some were utilized for background, while the transcripts of others were edited into several of the essays you see here. In the end, and without having to manipulate who was and was not included, the voices here represent a range of ranks, both officer and enlisted, as well as all branches and a variety of occupational specialties, times in service, duty stations, etc. Central to our work is that we felt it important, particularly as transgender voices have experienced significant marginalization, to let trans military service members speak for themselves. It should also be noted that one contributor has chosen to use a pseudonym.

In the following chapter, we provide an overview of transgender military service, generally, and recent policy changes affecting transgender military personnel. In chapters 2 through 5, we turn to the words of service members themselves. Chapter 2 contains stories contributed by veterans who left the service prior to Secretary Carter's 2016 announcement that transgender people would be able to serve openly. They share with us their experiences and their decisions to serve in silence. In chapters 3 through 5, we turn to the lives of those officers and enlisted personnel who, as of their writing, continue to serve. Some have transitioned, including having their gender marker changed with the military. Others are still navigating the waters to determine what will work best for them. We'll hear from service members like Zane Alvarez, a sergeant in the U.S. Army, who comes from a military family and enlisted just after his high school graduation. Sergeant Alvarez writes, "I'm here to do a job just like you. I'm here to be a part of this team, just like you. And nothing is going to stop me from continuing to move forward and serving with honor." We also hear from those such as Miranda Jones, a Marine Corps lieutenant colonel with thirty years of service, who has only recently begun to understand her gender identity. She joined the Marine Corps in early 1989, and her combat service includes two tours in Iraq and one in Afghanistan. We close with a chapter that responds to and reflects upon the experiences that have been shared, including the voices of several whose transgender identity prohibited them from serving.

PART I

Welcome to the Military

1

The Battle for Open Service

I was suffering so much as a person, as an airman, as just
some member of society and not being able to live as my one
hundred percent true self.
—Staff Sergeant Ashleigh Buch

When "Don't Ask, Don't Tell" was repealed, military-focused LGBT advocacy groups celebrated a major victory. Looking back, Andy Blevins, executive director of the Modern Military Association of America (MMAA) said, "We were ecstatic."[1] Although there was still much work to be done, they thought that major obstacles were now in the past and that everyone would be able to serve openly and authentically. However, a small portion of the lesbian, gay, bisexual, and transgender (LGBT) population wondered if they'd been forgotten. Department of Defense regulations would still discharge transgender service members if they were discovered to be trans. So, even as many lesbian, gay, and bisexual service members celebrated their newfound freedom, transgender service members continued serving in silence.

In July 2012, two of MMAA's predecessor organizations, OutServe, an "underground" support organization for LGBT service members, and Servicemembers Legal Defense Network (SLDN), providers of advocacy and legal defense for those discharged under DADT, came together to form OutServe-SLDN. When OutServe-SLDN named Allyson Robinson, a transgender veteran, as its executive director, many transgender service members grew hopeful that open transgender service would be better represented in their strategy. In an October 2012 interview, Robinson told BuzzFeed News, "I think a crucial part of that strategy is ensuring that the stories of transgender service members and veterans are being told. Having an organization like ours, that can help to elevate those stories and make them a part of the conversation, is very, very important. The more we tell those stories, the closer we are to winning that fight."[2]

Unfortunately, controversy struck OutServe-SLDN less than a year later, resulting in the resignation of Robinson and several other board members. But the "message" of storytelling had resonated with SPARTA, a separate organization that had emerged from OS Trans, a part of Out-Serve comprising transgender service members. SPARTA was composed of transgender service members and allies who positioned open transgender service as the spotlight issue of the organization, also providing members with support and resources while fighting for full equality protections within the military.

Among those moving from OutServe-SLDN to SPARTA were Sue Fulton, an Army veteran and a member of the first West Point class to admit women; Brynn Tannehill, a Navy veteran, helicopter pilot, and transgender advocate/author; and Allyson Robinson. Over the next few years, they would serve as the core drivers of SPARTA's policy initiatives. In a July 2013 statement about SPARTA's founding, Tannehill said, "We harbor no illusions that this will be a quick or easy process. However, our transgender group believes the people in SPARTA have the will, stamina, and ability to see this through to the end."[3]

During the first two years of SPARTA's existence, lesbian, gay, and bisexual allies and trans veterans were the critical and public face of the organization. Transgender service members could not, of course, be visible without risking discharge. By mid-2014, word of mouth resulted in over two hundred transgender service members joining SPARTA. However, while the organization's members wanted to tell their stories, they also needed to fiercely protect their identities. In 2014, nearly a dozen members were discharged for being trans, though it is important to note this was not because they had been identified as SPARTA members. At the same time, though, high-profile individuals and a series of events were changing the climate around trans service. Soon the spotlight would be able to shine on the accomplishments of the transgender service members themselves.

One notable activist was Kristin Beck, a recently retired Navy SEAL who publicly announced her transition and became an overnight sensation, drawing significant media coverage.[4] She drew attention to the fact that trans people were currently serving, even if they couldn't be recognized as such. The Palm Center, a research institute focused on sexual and gender minorities serving in the military, released a study in May 2014 concluding "not only that there is no compelling medical reason for the ban [on transgender service], but also that the ban itself is an expensive, damaging and unfair barrier to health care access for the approximately 15,450 transgender personnel who serve."[5] In June, *Time* magazine put actor and activist Laverne Cox on the cover and declared a "Transgender Tipping Point." Almost a year later, this was followed by Olympic decathlete and gold medalist Caitlyn Jenner's revelation that she was trans, reaching millions of Americans who otherwise might never have noticed transgender issues.

As society seemed to indicate a greater willingness to accept transgender people, attitudes inside the Pentagon were also beginning to shift. In May 2014, Secretary of Defense Chuck Hagel was the first to mention transgender policy as something at which DoD could take a look.[6] By December, Air Force Secretary Deborah Lee James came out in support of a change in policy. In February 2015, the new secretary of defense, Ashton Carter, visited Kandahar, Afghanistan, and held a town hall meeting with troops. Unbeknownst to Carter, Logan Ireland, a transgender airman, was in the crowd behind him and earlier had suggested a question to his doctor. That doctor, Navy Lieutenant Commander Jesse Ehrenfeld, now chair of the board of trustees of the American Medical Association, asked Carter about the ability of transgender people to serve in austere environments. Carter responded, "We want to make our conditions and experience of service as attractive as possible to our best people in our country. And I'm very open-minded about—otherwise about what their personal lives and proclivities are, provided they can do what we need them to do for us. That's the important criteria. I don't think anything but their suitability for service should preclude them."[7]

Secretary Carter's supportive statement was astonishing, indicating a significant reversal by the DoD. Asked about his reaction to the question having been asked, Ireland said, "The thought never entered my mind that the question would have acted like jet fuel for policy change."[8] On June 4, 2015, the *New York Times* released a short documentary titled "Transgender, at War and in Love," by director and producer Fiona Dawson. The documentary told the story of Ireland, deployed to Afghanistan at the time, and his fiancée, Laila Villaneuva, a transgender member of the U.S. Army. The documentary showed the capabilities of transgender personnel, even in an active combat zone, and highlighted many of the challenges they faced. Asked about what the film accomplished, Dawson said, "Logan and Laila's love story essentially helped reach people who wouldn't otherwise have paid attention to the issue."[9] It inspired discussion within the Pentagon, and on the day of its release the Air Force joined earlier announcements by the Army and Navy, stating in a press release that "[i]dentification as transgender, absent a record of poor duty performance, misconduct, or a medically disqualifying condition, is not a basis for involuntary separation."[10]

It was in this context that SPARTA's quiet and behind-the-scenes work within DoD really began to pay off. Sue Fulton, then serving as the president of SPARTA, and Allyson Robinson opened doors in the Pentagon that had previously been closed to such discussion. Transgender service members began making the rounds with senior military and civilian leaders to educate, allay fears, and show what a successful trans troop looked like. Navy Lieutenant Blake Dremann said of one visit, "The goal was to dispel any misconceptions around what trans service members looked like and how they served. It was by far the most important initiative that we worked. We trained people to tell their stories and put people in the spotlight."[11] The dividends were enormous. Ireland and Villaneuva were invited to the 2015 White House Pride celebration. In July, Secretary Carter announced a working group to study the potential approval of open service by transgender individuals. Carter said, "At my direction, the working group will start with the presumption that transgender persons can serve openly without adverse impact on military effectiveness and readiness," basically asking the Joint Chiefs to prove him wrong.[12]

The study ran six months, but other than a little-noticed policy announcement that Tricare (the military's health plan) would begin covering hormone replacement therapy, nothing regarding open service made the news. Meanwhile, SPARTA continued illustrating the competence and capability of trans service members, culminating in a meeting between Secretary Carter, Sue Fulton, and one trans service member from each military branch, each of whom wore the uniform of their true gender, not the one in which they had joined the military. Just as with the vast majority of earlier meetings, the secretary walked away impressed, but didn't reveal any plans. Navy Lieutenant Dremann, who attended the meeting, was sanguine and said, "We figured [open service] would happen during the summer of 2016. I honestly did not think Secretary Carter would let Pride month pass without announcing the change in policy."[13]

Many thought that an announcement would be made as part of DoD's Pride observance at the Pentagon, but Secretary Carter was a no-show and advocacy groups started to wonder what could be holding it up. Finally, though, on June 30 at the Pentagon, Carter announced that open service had arrived, saying, "Our mission is to defend this country, and we don't want barriers unrelated to a person's qualification to serve preventing us from recruiting or retaining the soldier, sailor, airman, or Marine who can best accomplish the mission."[14] With those words, he dismissed decades of arguments against trans service. Trans service members would be free to serve as their authentic selves.

As one might imagine, the mood in transgender organizations was one of ecstasy, accompanied by a huge sigh of relief. Organization leaders such as Blevins and Dremann anticipated that the next steps would be to deal with the challenges that come with any new policy implementation. Meanwhile SPARTA, now headed by newly promoted Lieutenant Commander Dremann, grew to over five hundred transgender members. As the need to protect identities waned, SPARTA's board of directors changed and was now composed entirely of trans service members or trans veterans. Carter's announcement also included a plan for the release of policy guidance and the beginning of training regarding the policy change. This was scheduled to run through July 2017, at which point the DoD would accept transgender recruits. The 2016 presidential election would dramatically change those plans.

Open transgender service had barely been in place four months when the election rolled around. The general consensus among LGBT advocates was that if Trump were elected it was going to get bad, probably very bad, but they also believed that trans service members would not be the first target. As a candidate, Trump had tweeted, "Thank you to the LGBT community! I will fight for you."[15] Sadly, that wasn't to be the case, and in the early days of the administration, the rights of sexual and gender minorities were rapidly rolled back in a variety of ways.[16] But, even with those events occurring, few thought he would go after transgender military service. Dremann said, "I figured there would be some hurdles added to service, but in the history of the DoD, policy [regarding inclusion of a minority group] had never been reversed after implementation."[17] Looking back, Blevins said, "I did not believe it would be as bad as it has been."[18]

No one expected the tweets of July 26, 2017. The United States was in a war of words with North Korea that was threating to turn into something worse. Most people would have thought that transgender military service was a low priority for the president. They were wrong. The president tweeted, "After consultation with my Generals and military experts, please be advised that the United States government will not accept or allow . . . ," but he didn't immediately continue. Many were concerned that the U.S. was about to go to war. Eventually, he continued, "[the United States government will not accept or allow] Transgender individuals to serve in any capacity in the U.S. Military. Our military must be focused on decisive and overwhelming victory and cannot be burdened with the tremendous medical costs and disruption that transgender in the military would entail. Thank you."[19] For trans service members, this was worse than a declaration of war. Going to war was something for which they had trained; this was not.

To this day, speculation abounds as to what caused the president to write those tweets. The Joint Chiefs reported being surprised by the announcement and explicitly stated that they had not been consulted. When asked about trans service several months earlier, Secretary of Defense James Mattis had said, "unless the service chief brings something to me where there has been a problem that has been proven—then I'm not going in with the idea that I am going to review these and right away, start rolling something back."[20] Evangelical leaders and the Heritage Foundation, however, were another story. Both had pushed a radically anti-trans agenda, which had raised suspicion that they were behind the president's tweets. And a group of House Republicans had asked for a reversal of the policy of inclusion in exchange for their support of a wall along the Mexican border, something the president had indicated was a major goal of his administration.

The "rationale" that really stuck in the public consciousness, however, was that of cost. Representative Robert Aderholt (R-AL) said, "This isn't about the transgender issue; it's about the taxpayer dollars going to pay for the surgery out of the defense budget."[21] From then on, critics of open service, including the president, would often point to fallacious information about the cost of medical care.

At that point, the only new data regarding transgender service was the one year of open and honorable service from transgender troops and all the service chiefs testifying before Congress that they had experienced no issues related to their integration into the force. Yet, a few days after the tweets, the president insisted that he was doing the military a favor by banning trans folks from the military. In a way, he was, perhaps, doing trans service members a favor as the spotlight shone on them far brighter than ever before. SPARTA, with help from other organizations such as OutServe-SLDN and American Military Partner Organization (AMPA), went into overdrive to reassure their members and to direct that spotlight onto those most capable of telling their stories.

SPARTA's president at the time, Lieutenant Commander Dremann, describes the immediate aftermath of the tweets.

> The beginning was chaos, absolute chaos. My phone exploded. I had no idea when taking over SPARTA that I would be thrust into the spotlight as *the* spokesperson for transgender service. We started by putting [trans] service members in front of the camera, telling their stories of service. We focused on their service and not their identity. SPARTA also avoided criticizing the chain of command, which is a big thing. All other organizations are free to criticize the President personally or Secretary Mattis. But we, as service members, cannot [and] that sets us apart. Our talking to the press is fundamentally different than any other advocacy organization because of our unique position as an active duty organization.[22]

Ashley Mack, then AMPA president, took the tweets personally and said, "He is going after my friends, friends I consider family. Once again, I had to turn this negativity into something positive."[23] The stories of honorable service, across every battlefield and occupational specialty, created a positive environment and had a huge impact on public opinion. Andy Blevins hailed the personal testimonies as critical, stating that they showed people that "trans service members are more like them than they realize. We are not dealing with mythological creatures here—we are dealing with your colleagues, and they are . . . here to serve the country they love while being true to themselves."[24]

Since a president's tweet is not the same as an executive order, it took time for the White House to officially transmit its intent to DoD and for DoD to determine what implementation would look like. DoD began by assembling a panel of "experts," consisting of the vice chiefs and under secretaries from each service, along with representation from the Office of the Secretary of Defense and various health and personnel organizations. At the time, these senior leaders were the exact same representatives whose work on the previous study had put open service in place. From SPARTA's perspective, the panel seemed initially a good thing as nine trans service members were invited to speak to the committee. "With the exception of a few individuals, the reception given to the service members was warm," recalls Lieutenant Colonel Bree Fram, one of the members called to speak.[25] Each member recounted their story of open service and answered a question or two, before being thanked for their service. Fram, as the most senior member present, spoke last and closed by stating, "The only thing we desire is to be treated like the soldiers, sailors, airmen, Marines (and Coast Guardsmen) that we are. We don't want special status; we don't want to be a different class of citizens. We want to serve."[26]

The panel heard from doctors, commanders of trans service members, and others. The thought was that maybe this was a way to shift the discourse and present an argument for retaining trans troops. However, the direction of the panel appeared to change when Anthony Kurta, an Obama appointee, was replaced as chair by the new under secretary of defense, Robert Wilkie, a staunch conservative who early in his career worked as an aide for senators Jesse Helms and Trent Lott. Thereafter, the panel focused on writing a report that contained talking points straight from the ultra-conservative Heritage Foundation and deeply anti-trans author Ryan Anderson. The report ultimately formed the basis for DoD's planned implementation of the president's ban.

In late summer 2017, an array of organizations, including OutServe-SLDN, Lambda Legal, National Center for Lesbian Rights, the Gender Justice League, and others launched four lawsuits against the proposed ban.[27] SPARTA assisted with finding plaintiffs for the legal challenges, but was not a party to them. In all four suits, district courts placed an injunction on the planned ban due to the immediate harm it would cause. One judge, Colleen Kollar-Kotelly, said, "On the record before the Court, there is absolutely no support for the claim that the ongoing service of transgender people would have any negative effect on the military at all. In fact, there is considerable evidence that it is the discharge and banning of such individuals that would have such effects."[28]

Litigation was one of the three ways the policy could be reversed to allow open service, and advocacy groups were determined to fight on all three fronts. The second front, in which any future administration could easily reverse the ban and return to the Carter policy, would have to wait until at least the next presidential election. The third was a legislative solution where open service would be enshrined in law. That method would require not only a continued public relations battle, but also one-on-one meetings with members of Congress.

In December 2017, five trans service members and veterans, Colonel (Ret.) Sherri Swokowski, Colonel (Ret.) Suzanne Wheeler, Major (Ret.) Kimberly Morris, Lieutenant Commander Dremann, and then Major Bree Fram briefed staff members from the Senate Armed Services Committee, held a meeting with the House LGBT Caucus staff and met with several senators. Even then, the feeling was that majorities in both chambers supported open service, but without changes in the leadership of the Republican-held chambers no vote that would rebuke the president would be held. Organizations would need to see a Democratic House and Senate or build a supermajority that could pressure Republican leadership into action.

In March 2018, the Pentagon released what came to be known as the "Mattis Plan," after former Secretary of Defense James Mattis. The plan's release brought another round of media attention for members of SPARTA. Lobbying work moved forward in fits and starts, but for most of 2018 things were at a standstill as the Mattis Plan had been blocked by injunctions and the cases before the courts were not going to be resolved quickly. Most analysts believed it would be eighteen to twenty-four months before any rulings came out of the courts. In the meantime, one particular part of the plan gave trans service members something to worry about.

The Mattis Plan contained a "grandfather" clause. At first glance this clause seemed innocuous as it would allow for anyone diagnosed with gender dysphoria by a military medical provider between June 30, 2016, and the effective date of implementation to continue serving and continue receiving needed medical care. However, there was a second, more insidious, clause that told the courts that if they found the service of grandfathered troops to be a rationale for finding the policy discriminatory and unconstitutional, the clause would be severed and trans service members who were already serving would be subject to dismissal. It felt like an executioner's axe suspended above the necks of trans troops.

By the end of 2018, after a midterm election put the House Democrats back in the majority, things were looking up. A legislative solution was back in play, as a majority of the House supported open trans service. However, a brief period of hope was shattered on January 22, 2019, when the U.S. Supreme Court ruled 5–4 that the government could implement the ban while the cases proceeded through the lower courts. In addition to asking that the ban be implemented, the Trump administration had also requested that the Supreme Court fast-track the arguments, allowing them to jump the courts of appeals and move directly from the district courts to the Supreme Court. The Court declined, ruling that the cases would proceed through the judicial system in the usual fashion. The decision was a huge setback for trans members, as they waited to see what the implemented policy would say and when it would begin. In response, SPARTA posted the following on social media, "We are disappointed in today's ruling. However, as service members, we are trained to continue to do our jobs to the best of our ability. We are in every combat zone where troops are currently serving, and we will stay the course as we serve our country with honor and dignity."[29]

With the opportunity to enforce the prohibitions, DoD argued that it wasn't really a ban, because transgender people could still serve, they just couldn't transition or seek any trans-related medical care. Several lawmakers decided to push back on these arguments, first by inviting several trans service members as their guests to the 2019 State of the Union address, and then by holding a House Armed Services Committee hearing on the proposed policy on February 27, 2019.

The hearing was split into two panels, the first featuring ground-breaking testimony from five transgender service members—Lieutenant Commander Dremann (Navy), Captain Jennifer Peace (Army), Captain Alivia Stehlik (Army), Staff Sergeant Patricia King (Army), Hospital Corpsman Third Class Akira Wyatt (Navy)—and Dr. Jesse Ehrenfeld. The second panel featured two representatives of the Department of Defense, James N. Stewart, acting under secretary of defense for personnel and readiness, and Vice Admiral Raquel Bono, director of the Defense Health Agency.

The service members faced a welcoming crowd, as the only Republican present was Trent Kelly, the ranking member of the Personnel Subcommittee. Even with overwhelming support, Lieutenant Commander Dremann said, "I was absolutely terrified testifying to Congress, but I wish more Republicans would have agreed to attend the meeting."[30] Much of the challenge regarding gaining acceptance is simply getting people to listen and see transgender people as human. A chance to speak directly with Republican lawmakers is a rare opportunity, and one that, in this case, was mostly missed. Had they taken the opportunity to hear directly from these trans service members, the optics of attacking actively serving members of the military would likely not have been good for the Republicans. Representative Kelly was respectful, and even appeared supportive of the service members at time, but he remained the lone Republican in attendance.

Representative Jackie Speier (D-CA), who chaired the hearing, said to the panelists, "Despite living in a nation where many discriminate against you, you made a choice that fewer and fewer Americans make. You joined the military and risked your lives and your family's well-being for our safety. And how has the administration thanked you? By treating you like a liability, not an asset."[31] From there, the panelists went on to describe exactly how they were assets to the nation, offering a litany of the contributions they had made both while deployed and at their home stations. They made the case that they were asking not for special treatment, but rather simply to be treated as any other member of the armed services. This included something provided to all other service members, the receipt of any medical care deemed necessary by their military health provider. In a fiery statement, Captain Peace went so far as saying that she would "be the first person to kick out a transgender service member if they are not able to meet the standards, if they are unable to deploy, engage and destroy the enemies of the United States."[32]

In an article published by ThinkProgress, Zack Ford recaps the second panel and its key moments as Representative Anthony Brown discussed with Acting Under Secretary Stewart why the current policy was, in fact, a ban. "Brown posed a hypothetical: If somebody showed up to enlist who had already undergone transition and was no longer experiencing gender, could they enlist? 'No,' Stewart replied. 'That's the ban. That is the ban!' Brown said."[33]

Acting Under Secretary Stewart and Vice Admiral Bono, however, attempted to double down. They claimed that the surgical procedures such a trans person might require are comparable to other disqualifying surgeries, like heart surgery. In other words, they directly compared being a happy, healthy transgender person who is otherwise qualified to serve with someone who has a debilitating condition. Representative Brown called out this blatant discrimination. Representative Speier attempted to follow up on Brown's questions. "You're talking, Mr. Stewart, of a health condition," she implored, noting that transitioning alleviates gender dysphoria and thus there is no comparable health condition. Stewart maintained that transitioning is just like other disqualifying surgeries. "You're not helping your case," Speier quipped back.[34]

Following the hearing, the House took substantive action and put language intended to restore open service into the National Defense Authorization Act (NDAA) for Fiscal Year 2020. Unfortunately, similar language was not in the Senate version of the bill and did not survive reconciling of the two versions before the president signed it into law. With the green light from the Supreme Court, neither the hearing nor the NDAA were able to prevent the Trump administration from putting the ban formally into place.

On March 9, a *New York Times* headline, "Transgender Troops Caught between a Welcoming Military and a Hostile Government," foreshadowed the upcoming policy implementation. In the accompanying article, Sterling Crutcher, a senior airman, described his personal experience serving while transgender, stating, "At my level, it's not an issue. I can meet and exceed all the standards, and the people I work with, they like me. They have a lot of questions, but they don't have a problem."[35]

Three days later, on March 12, 2019, the government unleashed its formal ban, "Directive-type Memorandum (DTM)-19–004—Military Service by Transgender Persons and Persons with Gender Dysphoria," effective April 12, 2019.[36] Any trans service member who did not have a gender dysphoria diagnosis in their military medical records by April 11 would be ineligible for any transition-related medical care. Although service members would be allowed to say "I'm trans" and access mental health care, they would be limited to serving in their "biological sex" and would be unable to transition. Transgender people attempting to join the military would be required to detransition (end or reverse one's gender transition, be that socially, legally, and/or medically), show long-term hormonal stability in their birth sex, and agree to serve under the standards (i.e., dress and appearance, fitness, and facilities) of that birth sex. Though the policy indicates that waivers can be granted, as of January 1, 2020, only one waiver was known to have been granted and that appears to have been a move to end a pending lawsuit challenging the ban.[37] It is worth noting that waiver authority is held at the level of the service secretary, a political appointee, and not by military medical or personnel professionals.

A number of service members faced a defining moment and, as the only way to preserve their career and future in the military, raced to get a diagnosis on their records. Groups like SPARTA, and a few heroic individuals like Captain Deirdre Hendricks and Chief Petty Officer Alice Ashton, did everything they could to provide matches between service members and doctors to facilitate those last-minute diagnoses.[38] Even then, mission requirements, such as deployments or flight status, prevented some service members from being seen before the deadline and a significant population of transgender service members who were unable to have a diagnosis placed in their records continue to serve, unable to do so as their authentic selves.

In the days before the ban went into place, trans service members were again at the U.S. Capitol, this time to educate and appeal to as many senators and representatives as they could. On April 10, 2019, the National Center for Transgender Equality led a rally on the National Mall to support trans troops. Following the rally, Lieutenant Commander Dremann and Lieutenant Colonel Fram provided remarks and held a press conference to discuss the topic. Though not enough to spur immediate action by Congress, the service members who fanned out across Capitol Hill, merely by their presence and willingness to engage, changed a few hearts on the topic of trans service, and perhaps on trans people in general. Perhaps the essays that follow will do so as well.

PART II

In Their Own Words

2

Serving in Silence

I would say the hardest decision that I've ever made, the most
traumatic decision in my life, was telling the Navy, "No. I'm
not coming back." And . . . not being able to tell the Navy why.
—Lieutenant Paula Neira

Sheri A. Swokowski, Colonel, U.S. Army National Guard, 1970–2004

Sitting in the third row of the auditorium the afternoon of June 5, 2014,
felt different from all of the other times I had been in the Pentagon. Earlier that day, I had been the keynote speaker at the Army Research Lab
in Adelphi, Maryland, sharing my transgender journey as part of their
Pride event. Now, I was back in the building attending the third Department of Defense Pride event since the repeal of "Don't Ask Don't Tell."
While a couple of hundred individuals were in attendance, there was
a distinct lack of senior leaders, the three- and four-star and flag officers that typically led each service. Perhaps the leadership had already
made their statement. After all, just two years earlier it had been standing room only with the secretary and all the service chiefs present at the
2012 inaugural event.

We waited patiently for the keynote speaker, newly appointed
deputy secretary of defense, Robert Work. He arrived after a twenty-
minute delay, apologized, and delivered his remarks. As I listened,
I keyed in on what he didn't acknowledge—the contributions of the
15,500 transgender members currently serving and the 134,000 transgender veterans who have honorably, and with distinction, served as
part of our military services. During his remarks, he addressed the
important contributions of lesbian, gay, and bisexual military person-

nel, but only mentioned transgender individuals when talking about civilians and stumbled when trying to draw distinctions between civilian and military personnel. You see, transgender personnel were not permitted to serve in the military, yet I and at least two other transgender veterans were in the room: Allyson Robinson, a West Point graduate, ordained Baptist minister, and, at the time, director of policy for SPARTA, and Kristin Beck, the former Navy SEAL whose story was told in the CNN documentary *Lady Valor*. The event emcee was another friend, Amanda Simpson, who was the highest-ranking, out, transgender civilian appointed by President Obama. Amanda is an awesome individual with degrees in engineering, physics, and aviation. Before transitioning, she was a test pilot for Raytheon Corporation. My, we seemed to be all over the place! Yet, we heard no mention of the value of transgender personnel in the U.S. military. In fact, a year prior I had received a written document from the DoD director of equal employment opportunity and diversity that denied our very existence within the military. The bottom line was that our military, after repealing "Don't Ask, Don't Tell" in 2011, continued to discriminate against its service members. Though we didn't realize it yet, in just two years hope would be on the horizon.

Although assigned male at birth, I knew from the age of five that I was different; I just didn't know what it was called. I admired my sister and always thought I should be wearing her dresses and skirts, and sometimes when I found myself alone at home, I did. Like many trans children, I prayed at night for God to fix His mistake; the next morning I realized He hadn't. The following night I would pray even harder. In the end, as a child of the fifties and sixties it was easier to conform to the conservative values of my Roman Catholic family and the conservative area in which I grew up, as well as the conservative era, generally. I suppressed my feelings and lived up to others' expectations instead of my own.

I was so adept at masquerading as male that I never experienced much of the bullying, taunting, and physical violence that many of my

LGBT brothers and sisters faced. To prove myself, shortly after high school I became a reserve deputy sheriff and joined the military, making the suppression of my authentic self a bit easier. In my twenties, thanks to articles about Renée Richards, a New York ophthalmologist and avid tennis player who had undergone a sex change operation and played professional tennis for five years, I finally figured things out. I now had a name for how I identified—transsexual, and later transgender, but that complicated things even more. By that time, I was well established in the military, had first risen to the rank of staff sergeant, then attended the Wisconsin Military Academy and earned a commission. Now I had the expectations of over eight hundred military folks, not to mention military policy, with which to deal. The stress of the new job, and my dysphoria, compelled me to experience brief interludes as my authentic self. I would purchase and dress in female clothing for a day or two. That was followed by feelings of extreme guilt as I purged everything I had just purchased, at least until the next time. And I knew there would be a next time, and a next, and a next.

While many discover that the military is not for them, I found that much like any other job, it is what you make it. The life skills I learned were invaluable, particularly during my road up to and including transition. Over the course of my career, I served at battalion and brigade levels, led a light infantry company, deployed twice, and taught with the Reserve Officers' Training Corps at the University of Wisconsin–Stevens Point (UWSP). Thereafter, I returned to the Joint Force Headquarters in Madison, Wisconsin, for a variety of interesting assignments. There I benefited from a couple of mentors who guided me through the later years of my military career. I then joined the Wisconsin Army National Guard, where I received several assignments that were rewarding both personally and professionally. Despite my career success, I continued to suppress my authentic self, interrupted by brief periods of authenticity.

As I approached the military retirement window, I felt safer about expressing myself as the person I knew I had always been. It took me fifty years, but I arrived at a point where I desperately needed to share things with someone. I had been married several times prior and had two children, but never discussed my "secret" with anyone. To do so would put my job, my family, and me in jeopardy. Now a glimmer of hope was approaching—the safety net of retiring with twenty years of active service. Although my spouse was a bit taken aback by my revelation, she made a sincere effort to understand. To her credit, she accompanied me to several regional transgender conferences, and we made friends with other couples in similar situations. She suggested the name Sheri and I chose that spelling because it combined female pronouns and myself (she, her, and I). My first public appearance as Sheri was while I was visiting Nevada. As my wife and I walked around the hotel and casino, I remember feeling every beat of my heart as if it were going to drive a hole through my chest wall. It was both terrifying and exhilarating! My wife and I lived a tenuous relationship, never sure where my need to be authentic would lead. I did know that my leadership experiences and the skills I honed in the military would serve me well in all future endeavors.

Retirement did little to ease the call to serve. In 2006, my former supervisor, one of my mentors, was on tour in Afghanistan. He mentioned that there was a vacant strategic planner position available at his location. I jumped at the chance to serve side by side again. I applied for the position as a government contractor and did not get that job. However, Military Personnel Resources, Inc. (MPRI) offered me a position as a lead course instructor at the U.S. Army Force Management School at Fort Belvoir, Virginia. I accepted the position and moved to the National Capital Region while my wife remained at her job in Madison. This proved to be a tipping point in my life. My hair was a bit long as I reported to work and some of the other faculty who were older, white, male retired officers joked about the new instructor being a bit of a "hippie." If they only knew the whole story; within just a year, they did. The freedom of living alone provided an opportunity for me to further explore my true self. I quickly developed a support group of trans women in the Washington, D.C., area and we saw each other often. The connecting place seemed to be our electrologist's office. As we all moved closer towards transition, I must have spent two hundred hours there having every hair follicle on my face (and elsewhere) burned away! Soon the only time I was male was while I was on the podium at the schoolhouse. The tight petals surrounding me were slowly being peeled back and Sheri was about to blossom. The path I needed to pursue became apparent. The question was how to proceed without hurting those I loved the most, my wife and family, and how it would affect my employment.

In the fall of 2007, I also came out to a couple of my mentors. I am sure they were a bit apprehensive when I invited them to lunch at my home, but our friendship over the years transcended the rough spots and it did not take them long to realize that the only thing that had changed was my exterior appearance; it now aligned with my internal sense of being. They communicated my change to agency leadership, who communicated it throughout the entire organization of about ten thousand people. Now everybody knew! In those early days, it was comforting to get calls from out of town and out of state from former colleagues who wanted me to know, personally, that I had their support. For others, it takes time. And sadly, for some there is not enough time. I once had lunch with a dear friend I have been close to for decades. We made it through the tough times of Officer Candidate School and worked together for twenty-five years afterwards. Yet over the past number of years my emails to him went unacknowledged. One of my mentors suggested I call him, and a few days later I did. We chatted briefly about having lunch and I sent him my contact information. After six weeks of not hearing from him, I figured the time still wasn't right. But thanks to the persistence of our mutual mentor, we finally arranged a lunch date. I tried to put myself in his shoes as he approached the table where I was seated. I knew it was difficult for him and I certainly understood the lack of eye contact during the first ten minutes of our conversation. After all, thanks to the hands of a skilled facial surgeon, I didn't look much like I used to! However, the conversation turned to families and friends, and suddenly he realized he was chatting with the same person he had known all these years. We chatted for two hours, just two retired infantry colonels, who had both turned pages in our lives. His comment as we left, "This was fun, we'll have to do it again soon," leads me to believe the next lunch will be even better.

Unfortunately, shortly after my very successful meeting with my old friend, I was fired from my lead instructor position. I should make it clear that the position was a civilian appointment and, as such, there was no bar to holding my position. Prior to my surgery I had duly informed the human resources (HR) director that I would be returning to work as Sheri. When she said that she had no experience with a transgender employee, I offered to meet with the staff, the faculty, and my counselor to educate and inform the employees. I was met with resistance. I should have seen this as a sign of things to come because on my first day back to work I was informed by my director, a retired three-star general who had served at the White House, that they had already hired my replacement. He admitted that I wasn't doing "anything criminal," but then kept the conversation focused on "my problem," my problem being my gender transition. I was amazed because I was still the same person doing the job, but I would soon join the ranks of the unemployed because my exterior appearance did not align with my employer's sense of propriety.

Shortly after being fired I went to work as an analyst at the Pentagon. One of the duties at which I excelled was representing the assistant chief of staff for installation management, a three-star general, every week at a secure, worldwide, strategic video teleconference. As the general's representative, I finally had a seat at the table. I didn't have to worry about securing one of the seventy seats available to everyone else. Although the DoD is perceived by many to be an extremely conservative environment, my experience there was very positive. It was professional, cordial, social, and based on my performance, not my appearance. I spent three years as the regional HR director for the U.S. Forest Service in Colorado before leaving federal service.

My original post-transition plan had been to blend into society but being fired as a government contractor for being who I am changed that! Since then, it's been about making things easier for those who follow. In

2008, I began working with then Representative Tammy Baldwin (D-WI) to secure basic civil rights for members of the LGBT community, with an emphasis on transgender rights. I travel to Washington, D.C., several times a year to advocate on Capitol Hill and elsewhere. We have made some progress over the years, but there is still much work to be done. In July 2014, I met with now Senator Baldwin in her Washington office. She reminisced that when we started working together only a handful of Congressional representatives had ever met a transgender individual. Now, she assured me, all 435 representatives have been visited by transgender constituents.

Over time, I learned that education is the key to ending the discrimination, bullying, and violence transgender individuals face. Sharing our stories is vitally important. While over 80 percent of the population knows someone who is gay, only 9 percent know someone they recognize to be transgender. But sharing our stories is difficult for most. After all, why would we risk the exposure to ridicule and scorn and to the opening of old wounds? Yet it's the lack of societal exposure and education that is literally killing us. We must increase that figure of 9 percent. We can't do it alone; we are too few, we need the support of allies. Mara Keisling, the executive director of the National Center for Transgender Equality (NCTE) in Washington, D.C., has said "When people get to know us, more often than not they find they like us."

Although the diagnosis is the same, each transgender journey is unique. My experiences, although delaying my authenticity to later in life, provided me with a solid set of skills that enabled me to transition relatively smoothly and to be successful at a high level. I consider myself to be extremely fortunate; but surviving and flourishing is not without costs, as I lost my marriage and family relationships along the way.

I probably did a few things well to attain the rank of colonel; however, I often wonder how much better a non-commissioned officer and commissioned officer I could have been had I been able to transition while serving. I am convinced our military leaders will soon realize the discrimination that exists and act to unleash the full potential of currently serving soldiers, sailors, airmen, and Marines. As I look back at the Pentagon Pride event, I am convinced that Deputy Secretary Work stumbled not because there was a difference in the categories he covered, but rather he realized there should be no difference in how all service members are treated.

Unfortunately, discrimination followed me well after my transition. In 2010, a U.S. Forest Service supervisor felt it necessary to bring to the attention of the hiring manager that the name on my DD 214 (Certificate of Release or Discharge from Active Duty) was different from that on my application. At that time, the Department of Defense had steadfastly refused to update transgender veterans' records of service. As a former HR director for two federal agencies, I can attest to the importance of an accurate DD 214 as part of any veteran's application packet. Fortunately, in 2014, DoD agreed to provide transgender veterans with updated DD 214 forms reflecting their post-transition names. My request was submitted in May 2014. On January 21, 2015, just two years after being informed in writing that we don't exist in the military, the Army Board for Correction of Military Records notified me they would be issuing a new DD 214 reflecting my legal name! As the highest-ranking out transgender veteran in the United States, and perhaps the world, I have and will continue to advance the fight for equality. The military teaches us to fight; DoD and other organizations shouldn't be surprised when we do.

Evan Young, Major, U.S. Army, 1989–2013

Underneath my headgear, I walk a straight line, returning salutes as I pass. A sergeant salutes and says, "Good morning, sir." A warm glow flushes my cheeks, and I reply, "Good morning!" Closer to work a familiar face draws near and salutes; "Good morning, ma'am." A heavy feeling of discontent weighs on me, and I return the salute with the grudging reply, "Good morning." I am transgender. At the time I was a military officer and, while I was not openly trans, I knew it to be so. Outside of work, I live my life as a man. Once on post, I am female. My short hair and manly features present an androgynous and confusing appearance.

I grew up in Arkansas and I knew that many outsiders perceived women there as "barefoot and pregnant" rednecks. That stereotype drove me to move out of state and join the Army. I wanted to be on equal footing with men. Along the way, I found new confidence as my drive to exceed expectations helped me rise through the ranks. Yet I always had the feeling of being a second-class soldier because of my gender.

Males have confidence ingrained in them at an early age. Men are encouraged to stand up for themselves and speak their mind. When they don't, they are often labeled effeminate or called derogatory terms such as "faggot" or "princess." This stereotypical "male" role is enforced by men as well as women. A woman speaking to a man who seems effeminate may treat him differently, too.

Because I was seen as a strong female, I was the target of intended slurs such as "tomboy" or "lesbian." Although I wore these labels proudly, I never felt as if I measured up to the boys in my class. As a female, I was encouraged by my parents to play sports and follow my interests in math and science. They were very supportive and allowed me to pursue what I wanted. Society, on the other hand, looked down on my pursuit of more stereotypically male interests. After all, women were expected to want to marry and have children. I always knew that I was not just a strong woman. I have "known" from an early age that one day I would grow up and be a man, but it wasn't until the past few years that I came to realize that I could actually do so.

Patriarchal dominance in society keeps many women from reaching their highest potential. In the military, denying women roles in combat ensured that men always held the positions of highest authority. Women were enshrined as something less, trapped beneath what some have referred to as the camouflage, rather than glass, ceiling. With the lifting of the ban on women in combat, this is now changing, but creating an environment in which young women have unlimited role models and opportunities will be a big part of ushering in the next generation of women leaders.

As a trans man, I recognize the male privilege I possess when I am recognized as male. I am seen as knowledgeable about the mechanics of my truck even if I have no clue what is causing my starter to not turn over. I can buy a new car without having someone try to pull the wool over my eyes. I can call the plumber, and he speaks with me as an equal. Writer Rebecca Solnit observed this too, writing, "Men explain things to me, and to other women, whether or not they know what they're talking about . . . every woman knows what I mean."

Internalized privilege generates the confidence that I exude when returning a salute after being called "sir," despite being labeled a female. As a man, I have no preconceived lack of ability. I can be called upon to run an operation without my superiors thinking I need help. Sometimes, I think all of this may be just in my head. Then again, I've seen this first-hand far too many times when male officers were chosen over me even though I was more qualified.

All that being true, it is important to make clear that I did not transition to gain male privilege. Inheriting male privilege is a by-product of transitioning from female to male. Hopefully, one day the world will rid itself of the patriarchal mindset. Women are different than men, but everyone should have the same opportunity to excel. Misogyny has no place in our military, and I am gratified that leadership has been moving to affirm this. In that moment where I am called "sir," though, I feel like I can take on the world.

Despite the gains I've experienced, explaining the past is difficult for anyone who is transgender. A lot of us go to great lengths to hide our gender history. After transitioning, we do not want others to know of our past because we want others to accept us for our new gender. But hiding one's background creates a whole new set of fears and anxieties. Stories of playing softball for your alma mater become blended with your brother's experiences playing baseball so you don't "out" yourself as transgender. Explaining how you busted your knee in high school football becomes a story about playing a powderpuff pickup game with friends. Sports are largely separated by gender. The same is true for the military. This will slowly change with women being allowed to serve in combat roles. Today, however, if you went to Marine Corps boot camp in San Diego it labels you as male since no women are sent there for training. You cannot talk about boot camp without exposing who you were—your gender assigned at birth—just as discussing your time on submarines or serving in the infantry would out you.

By gaining the male characteristics that I had always wanted, I lost my history as a woman. It is as if I never existed before my transition. I can no longer share some of my most joyous moments that expose me as having once lived my life as a woman. When someone asks where my daughters' mother is, I cringe and say it is complicated. I want to tell them that it was me that gave birth to them, but I choose to remain silent. In my silence, I feel guilty that I am doing a disservice to other transgender persons by remaining invisible and passing as male.

I do not voice my transgender status in my local community. It is a personal choice, and I have had to come to terms with it. It is not just me I have to think about, it is my family as well. Being transgender is still stigmatized in society. I know we need to change the hearts and minds of Americans, but the price to pay to make change happen is very steep. Since I am new to this town, I want to gain the community's respect before I come out. Beyond the city limits, though, I want my voice as a trans man to be heard.

At my daughters' school Valentine's Day party, red and pink hearts, balloons and streamers dotted the classroom. My Valentine's Day sweethearts are my twin daughters. I gave birth to them, yet I can no longer share that joyous moment with other mothers. While watching the kids pass out candy and cards, two mothers were talking about their pregnancy experiences. One spoke of how difficult her daughter was to deliver. The other said she had a pretty easy time. My thoughts raced; I wanted to connect with them, but how could I? I wanted to say having twins was amazing. I wanted to say I had a C-section and that they came early because the doctor accidentally induced early labor, but I didn't. I couldn't. I am Dad now and only a few people know that I was their mother. I tell people "we" had twins. I wanted to be a part of that "mom group," but could not.

A trans woman veteran named Paula told me, "Those of us who are no longer serving in uniform have an obligation to tell our histories truthfully if we ever hope to change the regulations for those who are in uniform and can't tell their truths. The public needs to know our stories and putting faces and real people on the issue of 'transgender service' will be vital to winning just as it was in repealing 'Don't Ask, Don't Tell.'" However, outing yourself is complicated at best.

A friend of mine, an active duty trans man in the Army, tries to embrace his past in hopes that it will help others that are questioning their gender. I'm trying to embrace myself and my past—both civilian and military, but when I tell people why I left [the military] and the rest of my story, it outs me. I want to come to terms with myself in every point of my life and am hoping that my story helps other people someday. Overall, though, being honest and open seems to be my best bet. I've gotten nothing but respect in return . . . nothing malicious yet. Explaining one's past is a personal choice, but the decision nonetheless causes a great deal of anxiety. I am still conflicted about choosing to lose my history as a woman. Hopefully, I will overcome my fears and embrace my past so others can see the true me.

I thought my journey began once I had a new name, but I was wrong. My true story begins on my medical retirement date after fifteen years of honorable service. Throughout my career, I won awards and received high marks for my dedicated and exceptional work; however, that was not enough to shield me from scrutiny. I have been the subject of two investigations, each desperate attempts by my commands to sabotage my career prior to the end of DADT. I've sat in a room with an investigator, a blank sheet of paper, and a pen while he pressured me to give up names of friends that I knew were gay. I refused. My command searched through my medical records, looking for proof of me being transgender. They found nothing definitive.

Being forced to live my life behind a mask left me frustrated with the military. I have faced harassment at every level of my career—a drill sergeant trying to take advantage of me in basic training, a first sergeant forcing himself on me as a lower enlisted person, a different homophobic first sergeant going on a crusade to have me kicked out for being gay, and a lieutenant colonel bent on proving that I was transgender. I have survived them all.

For me, there was no outlet in which to confide my secrets. Fear of repercussion sealed my lips. Today, there is a network of LGBT soldiers and allies to whom I can confide my frustration. Organizations such as the Modern Military Association of America provide a much-needed support system. I never trusted anyone during my military career, even psychiatrists or psychologists. Therapy simply proved that I had anxiety and depression, but the real reasons were never revealed.

Now that I am retired, I feel a tremendous weight lifted from my shoulders. I can be who I truly am and, more importantly, I no longer have to hide my family. As a single soldier, it was much easier to hide my feelings and blend in, but having children with my partner brought a whole other level to hiding who I am. Children will out you inadvertently, calling out for both moms at military family functions. Once I had kids, I could never bring my girlfriend to functions with my kids present.

I felt like even more of an outcast after a year of my secret transition to becoming male. It's not just me that suffered though. My children did as well. I chose to live far away from the military community in order to distance myself from prying eyes. At home, my neighbors have no clue that I was born a female. My children are young and unprejudiced enough that they accept me unconditionally. Since starting testosterone, my voice has dropped. With it, my children wanted to change from calling me Mommy to calling me Daddy. For them, it was a logical transition; I have a boy brain, and doctors are helping me have a boy outside. After a year into hormone replacement therapy, Daddy is a natural designation for them, but I continued avoiding military functions that encouraged family participation. Shopping at the commissary or post exchange with my kids was out of the question. The simple word "daddy" could have jeopardized my entire career.

Every day when I went to work, I left my secret life at the gate. The prohibition on transgender military service affected my career and my military family and, since I chose to stay away, I missed opportunities to build cohesiveness with my unit. Transgender discrimination hurt not only me and my family, it also hurt my military team. In the military, forming a bond with fellow soldiers means forming a family, but I didn't form that bond for fear of being outed as a lesbian or (now) trans man. Let me be clear, it's not the presence of transgender personnel the inhibits cohesion, but the ban on our presence. The repeal of DADT finally allowed me to bring my partner to events, yet I remain trapped behind a mask.

A. Jordan Blisk, Senior Airman, U.S. Air Force, 2011–2015

As a Midwestern-raised, bisexual, transgender Chinese adoptee, I often feel as though my intersectional identities are little more than a hypothetical caricature of leftist identity politics joked about by right-wing pundits. But I hope that, in sharing my story, others will be able to connect more deeply with pieces of their own, finding compassion and empathy for both of us in the recognition of shared, human struggles. My journey toward self-acceptance and authenticity has both benefited and suffered from the lack of predecessors who have walked the same roads I do. In many situations, not having the benefits of role models has left me flailing for direction and guidance. In others, I recognize my great good fortune in being able to define my own place in the world without some of the pressures and expectations that are inherited through more common social identities.

Growing up in Indiana, there was a clear expectation for me to attend college. However, though the expectation was clear, the financial logistics of getting there were far less so. My middle-class family was unable to sponsor my education, and the scholarships for which I qualified did little to defray the looming expenses of attending university. Thus, even though I was a reasonably good student in high school and my chances of university acceptance was promising, my ability to actually afford any degree program without incurring crippling debt was very limited.

As the fiscal realities of higher education began to set in, I also found myself embroiled in an escalating identity crisis over my sexuality. As tension continued to escalate between my emerging, irrepressible queerness and my restrictive, religious environment, I desperately began searching for a way to escape my homophobic hometown. In 2010, as a sixteen-year-old high school junior, I found myself at my local Air Force base, thumbing through recruiting pamphlets in the personnel office while I waited to update my dependent military identification card.

At the time, due to my sheltered upbringing, I had no concept of a transgender identity. Though I certainly didn't have a positive view of what it meant to be gay, lesbian, or bisexual, those terms' definitions were at least something I understood. In contrast, I thought that being transgender was simply a sexual fetish, perhaps just the result of extreme gayness. Though President Obama had signed a bill allowing gay, lesbian, and bisexual service members to serve openly without fear of discharge, I knew that my religious high school and church would kick me out in a heartbeat, and I was desperately afraid that my parents would too. Because, at the time, I was primarily attracted to women, I assumed my role as a closeted lesbian and silently began to plan my escape into the military. Not long after my seventeenth birthday, I signed my contract with the United States Air Force.

Less than two months before I was set to graduate from high school and ship out for basic military training at Lackland AFB in Texas, my escape plan nearly unraveled. I was outed to my church. I still don't know who did it, but I can never forget the result—my pastor ambushed me with his Bible open, readily and gleefully prepared to threaten me into penitence. Chronologically, he read me each and every passage about homosexuality, interspersing his recitations with demands that I repent for my sin. Over the following weeks, he and other church leaders relentlessly attacked me, telling me that I was past the point of no return with Jesus and that unless I turned back to God, I could never achieve any meaningful success or happiness in my work, education, or relationships. Ultimately, it was their threat to inform my parents and high school (which would have immediately expelled me as a matter of policy) that coerced me into feigning repentance just long enough for me to graduate, chop off all of my hair, and leave the state. Once they discovered my lie, I was excommunicated.

As I began my adult life a thousand miles away from home, the military provided small but consistent validations to a part of myself that I had attempted to eradicate through prayer and repression. Much to the chagrin of my mother and the older women of my church, my gender expression was stubbornly nonconforming, even as a child. However, in the military, the unflattering, nondescript nature of my new military uniforms relieved me from constantly offending sex stereotypes, and I finally felt free to distinguish myself through my personality and talents rather than through my consistent failures to be correctly female. My newfound freedoms unlocked a part of me that I had never been free to explore, and while I was puzzled by my strong urges to indulge them, I couldn't stop taking every opportunity to do so. The enormous sense of relief I felt as others exclusively referred to me by my rank and last name was as confusing as it was liberating.

When I found out that I could purchase certain "male" dress uniform items and wear them without violating Air Force regulations on "female" dress and appearance, I spent half of my paycheck on new uniform items, even though, as an aircraft mechanic, I knew I would have few actual opportunities to ever don them. I spent the other half of that paycheck on "male" civilian clothes, and it wasn't long before I began to unintentionally pass as a male in my interactions with strangers, at least until I spoke. I wasn't exactly comfortable with being read as male, but I was just as uncomfortable when others would "correct" themselves and use female pronouns. Without a framework to understand gender identity, I minimized and dismissed these experiences as merely a part of my burgeoning butch identity.

Though I was initially wary of coming out as a lesbian in the very new military environment post–"Don't Ask, Don't Tell," I eventually chose to do so. I cringed the first time I let the word "girlfriend" slip from my mouth in front of my flight, waiting for hostility and homophobia to erupt, but instead, I was shocked by the amount of respect and acceptance my peers showed towards me. With growing confidence in myself, I decided that, after a few months in training, it was time to come out to my family. At that point, I was financially independent and half a country away. I intentionally timed it to give them a few weeks to cool off before I returned to Indiana. When I finally made the call, I sat on my dorm bed and hastily blurted out the contents of a letter I had pre-prepared, immediately hung up the phone without giving them a chance to respond, and instantly burst into sobs. My roommate, a straight ally from California, just held me until I was done crying. Then she walked out of our room, reappearing a short time later with snacks and a DVD copy of 21 Jump Street to distract me from the bomb I had just detonated. Her acceptance inspired my own, and as time passed, my internalized shame and guilt began to fade into righteous anger towards those who had wronged me.

I spent the next year on active duty, learning my role as an aircraft fuels systems technician on KC-135(R) Stratotankers. As the first "female" to work in my fuels shop in a decade, for once, my masculinity became an asset. While I certainly experienced my share of sexist remarks, my gender presentation allowed me to escape the routine denigration targeted at other female mechanics whose traditional femininity prompted scrutiny as to their competence and technical proficiency. I also largely avoided the aggressive sexual harassment which often accompanied it, though I was not spared from race-based harassment.

During that year, my anger over my high school coming out experience steadily amplified. I was furious that I had been bullied by trusted authority figures, brokenhearted at the loss of almost my entire childhood community, and yet still terrified that their doomsday predictions for my future would prove true.

In response, I threw myself completely into my education, unsure of where it would take me, but desperately hoping that it would one day make me untouchable. While still on active duty, I enrolled as a full-time student at my local community college, completing my schoolwork around my full-time workdays, and studying for college-level exams to allow me to bypass low-level prerequisite classes. My hard work eventually paid off, and I was later able to enter my undergraduate university as a junior due to all the credits I had accumulated on active duty.

During my time in college, I continued serving in the military as a reservist and finally learned about the transgender community and gender identity for the first time. I remember feeling a rush of complex and terrifying emotions as I began to grapple with the reasons why identifying as a lesbian had never felt completely right to me. At first, I was in total denial. For a while, I successfully kept up a façade with everyone around me, including myself. To an extent, it was easy because I didn't have many external resources readily available to facilitate a gender transition anyway. There were no doctors in my city who could provide hormone replacement therapy (HRT), and I was only vaguely acquainted with one real-life trans person. But eventually, in early 2014, my curiosity led me to the online trans community, and it was there that I learned about the options for medical, legal, and social transition.

At the time, I didn't know what my next step was supposed to look like in any area of my life, and throwing a gender transition on top of my uncertainty felt impossibly overwhelming. I was absolutely terrified of coming out for a second time and risking the loss of my entire world again. Because I was still serving in the Air Force Reserves, I knew that coming out (or being outed again) would instantly rip away all of the educational stability I had fought so hard to secure. So, desperate to avoid further disturbances, I buried my feelings as deeply as I could and attempted to make myself forget the whole thing. It didn't take long to prove that course of action infeasible, and I quickly fell into a deep and worsening depression that closely mirrored the experiences I had when actively repressing my sexuality as a teenager. Ultimately, I was forced to answer a simple question: was being trans really worse than being dead?

In spite of my fear and hesitation, I decided to accept the risk of discharge and begin my transition. That choice seemed necessary, as I didn't think I could continue surviving the mounting dysphoria I was experiencing without a definite end date in sight. However, getting kicked out of the military was also nonnegotiable, as it would have taken away my means to transition. I needed something that would allow me to leave the military early but on good terms so that I could pursue my transition outside of its purview, and higher education seemed like the perfect solution. During my time as an undergraduate student, I had begun to recognize and yearn for the tremendous power that lawyers held as social architects charged with sculpting and defending the very framework of our nation. I wanted that power for myself and my community, so I poured every free second that I had into studying for the Law School Admission Test (LSAT) and preparing my applications. I hoped that law school, and the GI Bill benefits I had meticulously saved to pay for it, would be my final ticket out of Indiana. Despite civilian society's growing acceptance of transgender people, the military climate remained hostile to our existence, and I knew that I needed to get out of the Air Force. I figured that a cross-country move to attend law school would provide me with the cover I needed to escape before my medical transition became too obvious, so I planned to enter law school in the fall of 2015. In December of 2014, I graduated from college a year and a half ahead of schedule and had my first testosterone injection a week later.

When I finally received my law school admission letter and was offered a good scholarship from my first-choice school, the University of Colorado Law School, I started to see the first glimmer of hope that maybe, just maybe, I could rise above the dark predictions my high school pastor made about me. Over the following few months, thanks to testosterone, my voice dropped rapidly, and I quickly outgrew my uniforms. Because I was in the reserves, I was only on base for a few days each month, so it was easy enough to keep my mouth shut and play my raspy voice off as a several-months-long cold. However, I found myself living three starkly different lives. To my civilian coworkers, I was presumably just a cisgender, straight man. To the military and general society, I was presumably a cisgender, lesbian woman, albeit a gender nonconforming one. Only to my closest friends and in the comfort of my own home could I be honest about my identity as a trans man. The months I spent constantly and abruptly shifting through such differing social roles were confusing and stressful, but eventually, my final drill date came and went. In July of 2015, I left the military, moving to Colorado to become the first openly transgender student at CU Law.

Four years after hanging up my military uniform for the last time, I am overwhelmed with gratitude for my younger self for daring to have the self-awareness, courage, and resourcefulness to survive. There is much left to learn about the world, but I know that I have successfully carved a place for myself in it despite all odds. The military, for all of the challenges it brought, offered me a path to safety and stability and gave me the opportunity to surpass even my own wildest hopes and expectations.

Today, I am currently the only transgender attorney of color in Colorado, and though I still don't have a roadmap for my future, I do have the unique opportunity and a moral imperative to share my story for the benefit of those who will come after me. After soaking in shame for years over my sexuality, gender identity, and race, I am finally beginning to understand why the concept of pride is so meaningful to the LGBTQ+ community. Pride is central to reclaiming one's identity from shame. I am proud of who I am. My pride is not in simply having immutable characteristics that society has rejected me for, but because, through those experiences of rejection, I have forged a deeper connection to my authentic self, resilience beyond my wildest dreams, and something previously unfathomable: a persistent sense of hope.

Rachael Evelyn Booth, Petty Officer Second Class, U.S. Navy, 1969–1977

I was born in a tiny rural town in northwest Ohio in 1951. I joined the Navy right out of high school in 1969, serving until 1977. Because my parents couldn't afford to send me to college, it was a near certainty that, if I hadn't volunteered, I'd be drafted and sent to the jungles of Vietnam to shoot people and be shot at. I thought that joining the Navy would be my best chance to keep that from happening. It turned out to be the right choice. I joined because I had to; I joined because I felt it was my duty to serve my country; I joined to try to find a place in the male world where I could fit in as was expected of me. I am transgender.

I knew at the age of five that I was different—that I wasn't a boy—but I was forced to live as a boy by parents who knew nothing of how the mind could be a different gender than the physical anatomy of the body. I would sit in a small field behind our house every summer evening waiting to wish on the first star I saw to make me a girl. I loved helping my mother with cooking, cleaning, doing the laundry, and ironing. My stepfather drew the line at her teaching me how to knit. I learned early that how I felt inside made my daddy mad so I shouldn't say anything about it. It was a very lonely way to grow up. When I discovered that my new baby sister didn't have that little "thing" I had between my legs, my young brain came up with the only reasonable explanation: mine just hadn't fallen off yet. So I waited and hid my feelings until that magic moment came and I'd be a real girl. Of course, it took thirty-five years and was the magic of modern science, not of the first star.

When I realized at puberty that my body was going to rebel and make me into something irreparably *not* me, I decided that I was going to have to find a way to live in the male world even though I had nothing in common with the boys I knew. I disliked boys, but society wouldn't let me be friends with the other girls. So I made up my mind to somehow try to find some way to be a man.

While joining the Navy got me away from my tiny, backwoods Ohio town and opened the world to me, it did nothing to make my feelings of being "wrong" go away; it did exactly the opposite. I thought, while growing up, that boys were about two rungs on the evolutionary ladder below swine. In the Navy, I discovered that men were a few rungs lower than that. I couldn't relate to them and I couldn't stand being around them. But I now had no choice.

Boot camp was a real eye-opener, my very first peek into the world of men, and I didn't like it very much. They made me shave every morning. I didn't really have any facial hair—I was only seventeen and part Native American. But shaving forced me to admit I had a man's body and stimulated the hair growth enough that I quickly ended up needing to shave fuzz away each day. I hated the swearing, the exaggerated machismo, and the constant talk of women as purely sexual objects for men's enjoyment. I was appalled.

While in boot camp, it was discovered that I had an aptitude for foreign languages, so the Navy sent me to school to become a Mandarin Chinese and Arabic linguist. Being an interpreter, I was part of an elite force that didn't conform to normal Navy protocol. That is, we tended to treat each other as equals, regardless of rank and position. Although I was generally in the company of more intelligent men, that quickly turned out to be temporary. My job was to go out on board ships and intercept foreign military communications to learn of their defensive and offensive capabilities. That included having to have a Top-Secret Special Intelligence (TSSI) security clearance, which meant that my every move was constantly scrutinized to ensure I was worthy of carrying this enormous responsibility. During that time in the service, if it was discovered that you were gay you would be stripped of your TSSI clearance and kicked out of the Navy in disgrace. I wasn't gay and never had been, but if it had come out that I was transgender, it wouldn't have mattered. To most people at the time, there was no difference. No one really knew what the term "transgender" even meant. Letting my secret get out would have resulted in the same awful result. I hid myself.

On my eighteenth birthday, while in my first language school, friends discovered that I had never had a drink of anything containing alcohol. They bought me a pint of cheap whiskey, determined to get me drunk. They convinced me that I should drink the entire bottle. I became falling down drunk, alternately laughing and crying and finally blacking out. My friends delighted for years in telling me the things I did that night. I was horrified that I might have said something about my internal struggle, but no one ever said anything about it. I vowed never to lose control of myself again and after that night I never got drunk, never used drugs, and stayed away from religious groups. I didn't want to get caught up in something that I might have seen as a crutch to help me with my pain. Had I sought relief with alcohol, drugs, or religion, that would only mean one more thing I'd later have to overcome. I couldn't stand the thought of that.

I had thought that joining the Navy would let me find my place in the world. It started out badly. While language school was an incredible experience, being close in the company of men was not. I thought that marrying and becoming a husband would help. When I was nineteen, I married a woman. I was happy for a little while but being around a woman only brought out my jealousy for her body and her clothes. Then I thought being a father would be just the thing. I spent nine months green with envy that she was bearing our child instead of me. When I was attending school in Washington, D.C., for my second language, a local news channel began to show a week-long nightly segment about something that the hospital at nearby Johns Hopkins University was treating—transsexualism. I'd never heard the word. I stayed up late each night to watch the series that aired at the end of the 11 o'clock news. My wife thought it was "sick" and didn't like that I was interested in the subject. We ended up talking a little about how I'd felt as a child, but I convinced her that it wasn't a problem anymore. While we were overseas, though, our marriage broke up. I felt like my whole world was falling apart. I had failed at being a man in the Navy, I had failed at being a husband, and I had failed at being a father. I had nothing left. I thought of nothing but suicide for a very long time and was put on antidepressants. Our marriage lasted little more than a year and a half. She took our son and went back to the States. I didn't see my son again for eleven years.

Hiding my inner self in the Navy was an immensely difficult thing to do, especially when I had to go out to sea living on board ships with other men, bunking, showering, and working with them. On one occasion, the ship I was on had been at sea for several weeks and was scheduled to soon arrive at the next port. I was horrified to hear the men sitting around a table in the berthing area creating a little game they were all going to "play" when we arrived: they were going to have a contest to see who could do the most disgusting thing to the ugliest prostitute they could find. I was horrified to hear them laughing about this and finally couldn't control my anger any longer. I knew that one man was married, another had a fiancé back home, and another had a girlfriend that he was always talking about. I asked them how they could even think about doing something like this when their loved ones were waiting for them back home. They answered that "they had needs" and that their girlfriends and wives would never find out anyway. I asked them all, "What if *they* have the same needs?" One of the men looked at me and said, "She better damn well *not!*" His reply was abhorrent to me and he must have seen it in my face. That's when he asked why it mattered to me *what* he did. "What [are you], a faggot?" I realized suddenly that I should have stayed quiet. At that time, if you were on a ship and it was thought that you were gay, you could be beaten, raped, and then tossed overboard during the night. Nobody would realize that you were gone until the morning roll call when the ship would be hundreds of miles away from where you went over the side.

I left the group quickly and never made that mistake again. I can't describe how disgusted I was after we left port and they were all sharing their stories to see who won the contest. I ended up spending most of my time working so I didn't have to be around them.

Another big problem for me was the unfairness of the training we received. While women went through the same classes as the men to learn every aspect of the job we were expected to do, they were never allowed to go out on ships to actually do the job. Because of that, women had to stay back at the base, relegated to transcribing tape recordings made by their male counterparts who had returned from sea duty. It was horribly unfair. I took a risk and came out to a close female friend of mine who suffered this ignominy and we often found ourselves commiserating about it. I felt horribly guilty that I could go out to sea and she could not. She never turned me in for what I told her about myself, and we remain friends to this day. I later overheard a chief petty officer say that we only had Navy women at our station because the men needed company and that the local government in Spain where I was stationed had begun to complain that the American sailors were harassing the local women too much. During the 1970s, there was simply no equality in any of the country's armed services. For example, although the WAVES (Women Accepted for Volunteer Emergency Service) had been demobilized after World War II, the nickname "WAVES" for women in the Navy stuck. For years, Navy men found humor in the slogan, "Join the Navy and ride the WAVES."

The longer I served in the Navy, the more difficult my inner struggle became. Once, the Navy asked me to obtain my official birth certificate so that I could get a diplomatic passport for my work. The people in the personnel office looked at it and started laughing, pointing out that the letters "Fe" were clearly printed in the "Sex" box. Embarrassing as that was, I started to think that how I felt inside was somehow preordained fate. I had begun to buy women's clothing through the mail and had started cross-dressing in earnest whenever I could, always deathly afraid of being discovered by a friend who might stop by my apartment to visit. Then I met a young American woman whose father was a high-ranking enlisted man on the base, and we became very close. I came out to her one evening because I was sick of lying all the time. She listened intently and seemed very sympathetic. Her family was due to leave Spain soon and she had to leave but didn't want to do so. We came up with a plan: we would get married so she could stay, and she would help me learn how to dress and act as a woman so I could transition when I got out. Then we'd get divorced and go our separate ways. It was a dream come true.

She lied.

What she really meant was that she was going to "help me get it out of my system." When she realized that after I got out of the Navy I was seriously looking into starting to transition right away, she stopped taking birth control and we quickly got pregnant. Because my commitment to her surpassed my commitment to myself (I was terrified of moving forward), I put my own life on hold for hers and for our child. The marriage lasted nine years and we ended up with two children.

By 1990, I hated living a false life. I couldn't find the courage I needed to move forward, so I tried to commit suicide with pills. I failed, but it led to the realization that it wasn't courage I needed after all—it was conviction, the conviction that if I didn't do something, I was going to die. I made my decision to make the leap, and I never looked back.

There was one residual problem from my time in the Navy, though. For years, when I would tell people I was a Navy veteran of the Vietnam era, they'd ask if I ever went to sea. Since, at that time, women were not allowed on ships and I didn't want anyone to know that I had ever been anything but a woman, I would couch my answers in half-truths. I hated lying but I couldn't tell the truth without "outing" myself, so I would just answer in circles. I'd simply tell them that women couldn't serve on ships at the time. They would just assume that because I was a woman, I didn't go out on ships. It was a tightrope I continued to walk for a very long time, and it took a lot of mental energy to maintain.

I'm older now and I no longer play those games. I'm proud of who I am, I'm proud of being a Navy veteran, and I'm proud that I had the inner strength to finally become my true self. If someone asks about ship duty, I simply tell them I went. If they suddenly realize that women couldn't go to sea at the time, I tell them the truth about who I was—and that I got a lot better.

Danielle "Dani" Butler, Master Sergeant, U.S. Marine Corps, 1976–1998

Growing up I knew I loved wearing girls' clothes and often snuck away to wear them where no one else would know or see. I often dreamed of being made into a girl. But I always woke up, back to the broken me.

In my family, college was never a choice. The money just wasn't there, I'll leave it at that. I joined the military. Besides, I thought, maybe joining the military would fix me. A Marine recruiter was the first to talk to my parents, obtaining their signature the same month I turned seventeen, in December 1975. And that was how I ended up joining the Marines.

With open squad bays, cross-dressing was not an option during boot camp. I looked at it as I might have a prison term, knowing one day it would be over, one way or another. Not only did I survive, but I also received a meritorious promotion out of boot camp.

I then went to my initial occupational training, avoiding cross-dressing while living in a six-man room. That doesn't mean the desire wasn't there. I just didn't dare. Who would have understood? At this point in my life, *I* didn't understand.

I then went overseas, where I lived in a four-man room. What was nice was that we were all shift workers and would find ourselves in the room alone almost as often as we would be together. I learned how to cross-dress and sleep, cross-dressed, under my blankets during the day after working a night watch. I only knew that I enjoyed it. It felt right.

On one occasion we were having a JOB [junk on bunk] inspection and a woman master sergeant was inspecting my locker when she noticed panties in the top of my laundry bag. I thought I had hidden them better. When questioned as to what they were, I responded that they were "victory panties" from a date. I became popular for a while.

I was next assigned to a base in California, where I met my wife, another Marine. We hit if off so well. We were both very strong in our religious beliefs. I loved everything about my church. They believed what I was doing was wrong, which made me believe it was wrong, so I continued to hide my desire. We fell in love and, shortly thereafter, in January 1979 we were married in a Catholic service. Our first of four children was born in December of that same year.

Again, I was still a shift worker and often had time to myself where I would change into hidden clothes, even trying on some of my wife's clothing. No one ever knew and society still didn't want to know. I kept this to myself and enjoyed what time I could get to be me. I tried reaching out to groups like Tri-Ess, a support group for cross-dressers and their families, but they never responded. They were very tight and closed, not trusting outsiders. I don't blame them.

One trick I learned was to keep busy. A busy person doesn't have time to think. My wife and I led a normal life, as far as everyone was concerned, including my wife. I had an overseas tour, accompanied by my wife and son—and while there we added another son and daughter to the family. Later I undertook assignments as a weather observer and weather forecaster. Still, no one knew of the real me. I was getting higher in rank and had even started wearing women's undergarments under my male uniform. Again, it just felt right. I had told my wife that women's underwear was more comfortable, and I enjoyed it. She would try to find male underwear that was similar, but of course I would find something about the male version I didn't like.

One Friday in August 1988, I found myself reporting to the Marine Corps Recruiter Basic Course in San Diego, California. I was told to report to a classroom on a Sunday evening, wearing civilian attire. I didn't think anything of it. When I reported to the school, I learned that the reason we didn't have to be in uniform was they were doing a weigh-in. I was asked to strip to my skivvies. "Oh, Lord, what do I do now?" I thought to myself. I quickly turned to the instructor and requested permission to quickly return to my room for something I forgot. He asked what and without hesitation I answered honestly, my skivvies. He looked at me strangely and said, "Hurry up." Whew, I again avoided discovery. Such was life back in the military then.

I started learning more from the Internet. I was a cross-dresser. I found out there were others like me. And, I learned a new term, *pink fog*, a phrase I found on a cross-dresser website that meant dysphoria. I knew exactly what it was and what they were talking about! I had it so bad and so often! I would stay up late on Friday and Saturday nights so that I could dress as my authentic self. But we lived in military housing, and I could never step out the front door without jeopardizing my job or family's acceptance in the community. Nonetheless, even dressing in private helped me get by and enabled me to continue to serve in silence.

I then had an unaccompanied tour overseas; that is, my family remained stateside. Because I was now a staff sergeant and treated like an adult in the military, I was living in a room by myself with my own little kitchen and bath. I could get a couple days off and live as the authentic me for the entire time. I had also become braver and started underdressing more, even when in uniform. Upon returning to my family and the States I went back to how I had managed earlier, late Saturday nights dressed in my computer room. At this point I was involved in an accident where a tent beam fell and hit me on the head. It crushed three lumbar discs and caused a bubble in my spinal fluid in the thoracic region of my spine, a syrinx. This syrinx was causing me chest pain but was inoperable. So the military doctors put me on a medication for neurogenic pain, an antidepressant. The pain was controlled, *and* I didn't find life as difficult to deal with. One medication helped with two issues.

In 1998, I retired from the Marine Corps, having served twenty-two years on active duty. No one knew the real me, and even then I don't think I knew. I was never allowed to be the real me. Never allowed to even try to be the real me. Had I been allowed I am sure I would have been so much more productive. I would not have had periods of depression. I would not have taken my anger out on others or my children. I will always regret those moments. Because of others' misunderstanding, prejudice, hate, whatever it was, my life was greatly affected. My family's life was affected. And our government lost out on a person who could have been so much more productive if only allowed to express their genuine self.

In retirement from the Corps, I took a job working as a contractor for the Army, where I continue to work. My company knows about me and around my coworkers I can be me, but I don't do that around the Army. I've seen friends who came out fully while working as contractors be told they were no longer needed when the contract was renewed, with no reason. This is normal in the contracting world. Our world needs to grow up.

In 2017, I was able to attend a transgender conference, spending an entire week with others as a woman. It was only then, on my way home, that I realized how I wanted to live my life. I cried almost all the way home because I didn't want to return to the male me, even though I did look forward to returning to the love of my life, my wife.

It was after that conference that my wife confronted me and asked if I thought I was transgender. I responded like it was a dumb question. I thought it was obvious. I should have thought that one out more. My wife informed me that she felt that our marriage was based on a lie. She said that she had married me thinking I was a man, told me how she had mothered our children thinking I was a man, and on and on. All I could do was sit there, understand, and shake my head in agreement. All I could say was "I do love you." I then offered to shoot my brains out if it would help. She then realized how badly I felt, realizing it was hard on me, too. I explained how I had thought that marrying her might fix me, how having children might fix me. I explained how I tried to be "the man" everyone told me I had to be. My wife and I agreed on one thing after that discussion: I needed to see a doctor and get help.

I went to the doctor and explained how I had increased my pain meds as I knew it was an antidepressant that was also helping with what I was going through regarding gender. The doctor didn't like that and changed my meds. That is when my life really turned for the better. I was diagnosed with gender dysphoria. It would still be eight more months before my wife would venture out with the female version of me, but I took my time and waited for her to be ready. In January 2019, we celebrated forty years of marriage. The night before our anniversary, we enjoyed a girl's night out. She now supports me and my friends. With her knowledge and support, I am on HRT. Thank God society has changed, or I probably wouldn't be alive.

I served with pride for a country I loved, a country where I was willing to give my life in its defense. But I had to serve in silence. I was not allowed to be the real me and to some extent I am still restricted. Not everyone understands, I get that. If only they walked a short distance in my boots.

Hanna Tripp, Senior Airman, U.S. Air Force, 2009–2013

I believe in this country. For all its flaws, as I thought about joining the service, I saw the ideas propagated by the American ethos worth protecting. Growing up, I had witnessed these same ideals inspire this nation's most marginalized people to lay down their lives in the hope of advancing the freedoms that serve as the foundation of our democracy. I was not ignorant to the realities of the war I would be joining, but still, I harbored a belief that I too might be able to contribute some measure of good through my service. Though labeled as such I knew I was not a man. My decision to enlist was divorced from any notion of trying to "prove my masculinity" and was instead rooted, probably naively, in a sincere desire to serve. This was my reality of being a closeted transgender airman in the United States Air Force.

The irony of my story resides in how little being transgender influenced my service. Indeed, even after transitioning, gender is still a small part in how I identify myself. As recent debates continue about the effectiveness of transgender service members, I find myself longing to be back in Iraq. This is not a new feeling. For me, the ability to have a singular purpose that is so well-defined was unique to that environment. It was this environment that fostered a unity that made irrelevant everything except your ability to accomplish the mission. In this way, being deployed was liberating as I had no obligation to be anything other than someone who was able to accomplish the mission.

Showing up at flight school was an intimidating prospect. I learned early on that the program had a high attrition rate, be it from health, personality, or lack of requisite skills. I tried to prepare and sought counsel from those I already knew that had completed the program. Regardless of their status in the squadron, the one seminal theme echoed was "Don't suck." I recognize the inequalities that existed at the time—and, with the last vestiges of the "good ole boys club" still in place, do now—but in my squadron I witnessed a diversity that I had not yet seen anywhere else in the military.

While service members were still being penalized under "Don't Ask, Don't Tell," there were several aviators in the squadron who were known to be gay or lesbian. But, as far as I could tell, each was fully accepted as one of our own. While in the squadron, I had two commanders; first a woman and then an African American man, and crew members of every conceivable background who were united under the universal truth of "Don't suck." An innocuous and seemingly self-evident phrase that came to represent an egalitarianism that I have not yet seen replicated elsewhere. The same standard was expected of everyone.

Though I could not have readily defined it at the time, throughout my service I was cognizant that I was transgender. However, this was only one part of who I was (am) and I felt that my obligations to the people with whom I served and to this country superseded these feelings. Beyond that, I truly loved flying. Flipping switches in flight and experiencing the world at altitude never seemed to lose its luster; it was cathartic. There was a struggle inside me derived from the notion that my gender seemed to be instinctively wrong, but these feelings were ill defined and seemingly not worth the risk of exploring; so, I didn't. To confront this ambiguity required a courage that I had not yet learned to possess. There is a certain false comfort in the familiar.

Truth be told, I was also afraid of sharing this part of me, not from a sense of self-preservation or even of my job but of losing the trust of my peers. My greatest fear while deployed, or even flying, was not of my own personal safety, but of doing something that endangered the lives of my fellow crew members. There was a strange dichotomy with flying, in that no matter how much disdain might be harbored between individuals on the ground, the second we stepped on the aircraft together, any animosity became superfluous. Our duty to protect service members on the ground was a communal obligation that transcended any personal conflict or prejudice. Everyone was prepared to lay down their lives to achieve the mission. This was not vain rhetoric. I recall flying to a TIC [troops in contact—with hostile enemy forces] with one of our four engines disabled; the crew discussion centered only on the logistics of making it to the area of responsibility.

One of the fundamental mantras of aviation is that "there is no rank on the aircraft." Your authority comes from your crew position and experience. In an organization that is typified by its hierarchy of rank, the independence that this represented was not easily earned and, having proved myself worthy enough to be trusted with the lives of others, I was reticent to do anything that would jeopardize this faith. One would think that entrusting your life to another represents the ultimate bond, but at the time the mere notion of being anything other than Hugh seemed liked the exception. Growing up there was a narrative that a trans woman needed to ascribe to some superficial stereotype of gender. That was not reflective of who I was and was certainly not how I wanted to be seen. Trans represents so many things to so many different people that I honestly don't really want those definitions thrust upon me. Knowing that I am trans gives you almost no insight into who I really am. Unfortunately, once labeled your true personality can be obscured by the prejudices that people hold.

As a consequence, to admit being trans felt like a betrayal to those who possessed so much faith in me. The feeling was so strong that even after being out of the military for over six years, most of those with whom who I served are completely ignorant of my transition. I just couldn't confide in them. My lack of trust is, perhaps, misplaced in that everyone to whom I have come out has astonishingly been unfazed. The most hostile reaction came from a friend who expressed his disappointment, not because I was trans, but because in trying to hide it I didn't visit him while traveling in his area. Though transitioning while in the service would almost certainly have cost me the job that I loved, it seemingly would not have diminished the bond I had with those I served and with whom I flew.

During my first return from Afghanistan, we were accompanying a fallen service member and his wife. Both service members, they had been deployed at the same time. Arriving at Dover Air Force Base, we carried his body out of the aircraft, the grieving family who met us vocalizing our own emotions as this soldier's wife looked on stoically. In that moment I recognized within that woman the duality of being a service member who remained steadfast in her traditions, while her eyes betrayed a sorrow that surpassed any outward grief. This contrast struck me because I understood well the tension between being devoted to one's country, while also struggling to understand the institution of the military. In my case, it was a matter of feeling devotion to country while also feeling firsthand the discrimination that has long pervaded the institution. Despite the gravity of her loss, something within this soldier compelled a continued devotion to this country. Similarly, though not to equate death with discrimination, I felt both oppressed, yet proud of my service.

In writing this account, there has been a fine line between recounting my story and ensuring that I do not minimize the experiences of those who have suffered at the hands of this institution. I fully appreciate the disdain that our military evokes and, reflecting back, there exists a strange dichotomy in knowing the horrors inherent to the service while possessing the longing to be back in the air flying. While in the Air Force, I was a distinguished graduate in flight school, flew twenty combat missions in Iraq, and earned numerous accolades. I do not believe that I did anything less than what was expected of me. I mention this only to demonstrate that being trans did not affect my capacity to serve. Like so many other disenfranchised populations, I fought for rights in which I myself am not entitled, yet the foundations of our democracy instilled a belief, that despite its imperfections, it was worth defending. It's not that I wish to perpetuate those imperfections, but I do have faith in our country's ability to move towards the promise of equality for all.

3

Serving with Honor

We don't define ourselves on the fact that we are transgender,
but on the pride of purpose we put into our jobs.
—Staff Sergeant Aylanna Anderson

**Bree Fram, Lieutenant Colonel, U.S. Air Force/Space Force,
2003–present**

On June 30, 2016, sitting at my Pentagon desk, I should have been
focusing on how many satellites the Air Force could fit into its
five-year plan, but I had spent the past thirty minutes watching the
secretary of defense speak. When he wrapped up, I was nervous as I'd
ever been. Nothing in my fourteen years of service prepared me for
what I was about to do. My mouse hovered over a button labeled "post"
for many seconds. Eventually, I clicked. The world knew. I moved to
another button labeled "send" where the people sitting around me,
and many other friends and colleagues, were listed in the "To:" field.
I clicked again.

Here's much of the note I unleashed:

I want to share something with all of you. I'm transgender.

I've known I was trans since an early age though I struggled to find
the courage to admit what it meant to me and how I could, and would,
express myself. I no longer have any reason to hide who I am.

So why bring this into the open now? (Or ever?) With . . . today's just-
announced removal of the ban on being trans in the military there's really
no better time. As SecDef just said "Our military and our nation will be
stronger" with this change. I've done outreach events and advocacy work,

but I can have a lot more impact if my story is public. I want to be in position to help others and visibility is ridiculously important.

If my story can sway a few people from neutral to supportive on transgender rights or educate some folks who never had a reason to be involved or informed, I'd consider coming out to be a great success.

Peg and I want to raise the kids to be open, honest, and tolerant. They've known about me for a while as we felt it best not to lie or hide things from them that they would learn about eventually. We want to avoid any perceived hypocrisy between how we ask them to behave and how we behave. There will no longer be a need for worrying about who might know, or what can be said. None of this has been easy on her, and it probably never will be. Dealing with me being trans has probably been even more of a challenge for her than it has for me even though she's known since shortly after we started dating. She's been beyond amazing, even though it's been a total roller-coaster.

Day-to-day, this . . . frees us to be more open and effective champions of issues that affect us and our many friends. Perhaps I'm the first transgender person you know. If so, great! I'm more than happy to answer any questions about my situation or the advocacy work I've done. I'd also gladly share resources on transgender issues.

* * *

Not having the emotional reserve to stick around, I grabbed my gym bag and flew out the door. I didn't know what to expect when I returned to my desk, but the reaction far exceeded my wildest expectations. One by one, the people I worked with walked over to me, shook my hand, and said, "It's an honor to serve with you." I was near tears because they had it backward, it was my distinct honor to serve with them. It wasn't all rosy, though, as Peg lost a few friends and family members who couldn't deal with it. I was elated at my fortune, but deeply saddened by hers. How and why would people cut ties with her for something not even of her doing?

I figured I'd get right back to planning the future Air Force, but life took a twist. A week later my organization got a new two-star general.

On his second day I was in his office for an hour and a half talking about transgender issues. I'd never spent more than five minutes with a general and they were miserable "career counseling" experiences. This was different; he listened. As a fighter pilot, he related his experiences from the "Don't Ask, Don't Tell" era where everyone knew who was gay, but it didn't matter. What mattered was that the person flying on your wing was capable of executing the mission. Everyone took care of each other, because without mutual trust the mission would fail. Many people in the Air Force say, "Mission First, People Always," because if you don't have the people you'll never get the job done. The general took the same attitude towards transgender service. I was thrilled to have someone with that level of savvy in my corner. A week later I got a call from him asking if I wanted to switch jobs and serve as his executive officer. An exec gig is not easy, but this was a no-brainer. I was probably the first person in the armed forces to be offered a job *because* I was transgender.

Life was different after coming out; I was able to bring my whole self to work. The filter that had been installed between my thoughts and my words was gone. No longer did I censor myself when asked simple questions like "What did you do this weekend?" when the answer may have given away that I was transgender. I could now freely discuss topics that I had been afraid to get into for fear of where they would lead. The filter did have limits; if it was important enough I'd find a way to work past it.

One of those important moments came in 2015 while I served as a military legislative fellow on the staff of Congresswoman Madeleine Bordallo. In spring the topic of transgender service came up because Congress was considering if they wanted to prevent DoD from removing the ban. One of my friends worked for the committee with jurisdiction over policy-change legislation. We chatted, and I shared many reasons why open service could be so valuable. My friend took me aside and asked how I knew so much about the topic. The filter quickly engaged and my stress level spiked, but this was too important. I said, "Let me tell you a little something about myself . . . ." He was the fourth person I ever told I was transgender and was the perfect audience: relatively uninformed, but willing to listen before passing judgement. I gave him a lot to think about. I can't say for sure what came of it, but there were no more whispers of a legislative ban.

In 2017 the filter was greatly diminished with a year of open service behind us. On July 26, I was sitting in a cabin in northern Minnesota watching a family of ducks on the placid water as my phone erupted with a flurry of messages, many of which were asking if I was okay. I quickly found the presidential tweets and was shocked. I asked, "Why?" What could have caused this and what did it mean? After a talk from the administration of making our military more lethal and ready, the tweets resolved to do the opposite in removing thousands of well-trained service members. I knew a tweet wasn't policy, but the first shot of a long war had just been fired. A few months after the tweets identified me as a burden on the military, the Air Force placed significant trust in me by selecting me for command. I was excited but nervous to lead research and development of cyberspace and counter-drone operations. Part of the nerves were that I had never worked in that field, but luckily it was less about technical acumen and more about leadership. The significant nerves involved moving to a rural area as a transgender commander. It's common practice for people to google the new commander, so there was no way to hide who I was even if I wanted to. I had to embrace it.

Shortly before moving to my new position, I was promoted to lieutenant colonel at the National Archives. Congresswoman Bordallo swore me in as we stood in front of an original copy of the Constitution and I repeated my oath to support and defend the ideals enshrined in that document. That act felt incredibly reassuring because it wasn't an act of allegiance to a commander in chief, but to the freedoms that bind us together.

Soon I had to face the issue of how to come out again and do it in a way that didn't make me a distraction. In my first staff meeting, I discussed why a culture of diversity and inclusion contributes to mission accomplishment. I mentioned who I was as a transgender person and why that didn't matter at work, reinforcing that we're valued for what we bring to the team in commitment and competence.

In early 2019, the administration was allowed to implement the ban on transgender people by the Supreme Court. DoD started arguing that it wasn't really a ban, because transgender people could still serve, they just couldn't medically transition. My analogy for why some transgender people need medical care and some don't is that it's somewhat like monitoring cholesterol. If it gets to a certain level, you may decide to treat it; if it gets to a higher level or you have some sort of critical issue like a heart attack, you'd better treat it immediately. Gender is somewhat the same way; there's a threshold to transition. There are many factors that may keep some people back, but if they hit that threshold, it's time. Some people are past it before they can even express themselves, others not until late in life, and some never get there but are still trans. None of them are "better" or more authentic than any other.

If I hit that threshold after the ban was in place, I would immediately be ineligible for service even though it had no bearing on my capability. It brutalized me to think that my example of service as a trans person who hadn't yet taken what DoD considered to be transition steps could be the fig leaf on the policy that was all the Supreme Court needed to decide that it's constitutional and nondiscriminatory.

March arrived and though I continued to receive the unwavering support of my Air Force, the government announced its formal ban on the twelfth. Anyone without a diagnosis of gender dysphoria in their military medical record prior to April 12 who sought transition-related care would be subject to discharge. I was heartbroken.

This was the "Speak now, or forever hold your peace" moment. My crystal ball regarding transition had always been cloudy, but there wasn't any more time for the fog to dissipate. I previously strongly resisted the diagnosis, because a required component was that you had to have associated "clinically significant distress." The definition of that is open to interpretation, but I hadn't been willing to countenance something in my records that suggested significant distress. What did that say about me? Wasn't I good enough? Was I broken?

I wondered if it was time. Had I reached that threshold? Though I didn't feel like I was hard up against the female end of the gender spectrum, had my sense of self reached the point where it was time to change the "base model"? Peg and I agreed that it was probably better to be safe and get the diagnosis, since we didn't know how long this policy was going to be in place.

Work whisked me to D.C. on a gorgeous day and I was able to do my favorite spirit renewing activity: running from the Pentagon to visit the Lincoln and MLK memorials. They always inspired faith that a better future lies ahead. That night, I attended a dinner for counter-drone experts at a D.C. officers' club. As I threw on a sport coat, I looked in the mirror and was struck that this wasn't me. While it wasn't viscerally wrong, it wasn't right. I attended the meeting and did my job, though I was thinking about how it might be different in the future. I'd made my decision. With the gender dysphoria diagnosis about to go on my record, I was going to pursue an in-service transition.

On April 2, my civilian doctor diagnosed me with gender dysphoria and by April 5, less than a week before the deadline, I was informed by the Air Force that I was EXEMPT from the upcoming policy and I'd be grandfathered into the old policy. An enormous relief, but there were still so many unanswered questions about my future and the circumstances surrounding a transition. Peg and I had so much to work through between us, because who I am challenges and changes not only perception of me, but the world's perception of us as a family and her as an individual. When this came to light, would she lose more friends and family? What did it mean for our future, and . . . did we have a future together?

As the ban slammed into place on April 12, we were halfway through driving from New York to Minnesota to attend a grandparent's birthday party. We arrived and found my grandfather wasn't doing well and had moved to a hospice. I hadn't planned to see him until the next day but thought it best to go that evening.

My grandfather was one of the biggest supporters of my decision to join the military. He escaped Germany in the 1930s, was the youngest first sergeant in Europe in World War II, was yelled at by Patton to "Get my goddamn tanks moving faster!" and participated in the liberation of concentration camps. When I was commissioned, he was the first to salute me. He never failed to let me know how proud he was of me. As they hang proudly in my office, his two Bronze Stars and a picture of my other grandfather, an Army lieutenant who captured the city of Solingen, Germany, with guile rather than firing a shot are constant reminders of my family's history of service.

I got to his bedside and grabbed his hand. He opened his eyes, said my name, and a huge smile crossed his face before he fell back into a drug induced haze. I sat with him, and when I grabbed his hand to say goodbye, he swam to consciousness for a few seconds to look at me, smile again, and very clearly say, "Keep doing what you're doing" before he was once again pulled under.

He died the following morning, two days after a ban on service of people like me had gone into place. What if that ban had been on Jews like my grandparents? What would we have lost by discriminating? How much less effective would our military be without the service of African Americans, women, LGB service members, and every other minority that faced the same arguments that are now being thrown against transgender service members? I would be doing a disservice to all of them to not keep "doing what I'm doing" and fighting for the ability of all qualified Americans to serve their country and the ideals represented in the Constitution that we swear an oath to defend.

I was asked to give the eulogy at his funeral on behalf of his many grandchildren and great-grandchildren. For inspiration, I looked around his office. Proudly displayed next to a shadow box of his WWII memorabilia, I found the squadron coin I gave him on the day I was commissioned in 2003. I had my themes for the eulogy: the pride he took in all of us, his joy in seeing what his family turned into after escaping the darkness in Germany, and a legacy of service. Through tears, I spoke about the freedoms we enjoy today because of people like him who were willing to fight when darkness threatened. They recognized evil and stood up to it; may we all be so courageous. His final message, to keep doing what we're doing, is to all of us fighting for a better world.

Seth Stang, Staff Sergeant, U.S. Air Force, 2010–present

Being "grandfathered" in. I never knew that term would hold so much meaning in my life. On the one side of it I'm happy to have made it through the military transgender ban, on the other there are so many of my friends who didn't. It's like being on a lifeboat and having to watch as the rest of your friends go down with the ship. I've heard things like, "You made it," and "I'm glad you survived." My friends and family talk about it like a mass execution and, in a small way, perhaps it is. Not the ending of physical lives, but a stamping out of a group of people. The erasure of a minority whose only sin was being themselves, their very existence making them pariahs marked for removal.

It's not the first time I've been banned from something. I was banned from marriage, banned from expressing my sexuality, even banned from my home as a teen. The thing that hurt most this time though was that this ban, this new rejection, came after I had been told I was accepted. For the first time, I, and others like me, were welcomed to be who we truly were and were told to come out from our hiding places. We dropped our walls and, a short time later, they dropped the bombs.

I was twelve years old when I first learned the term "transgender." My parents and I used to watch shows on the National Geographic channel. One episode featured "India's third gender." That episode changed my life as, for the first time, I realized I didn't want to *act* like a boy—I *was* a boy. Up to that point, all of the common excuses had been made. "I was just a tomboy," "girls can like boy toys, too," "it's just a phase." I wouldn't come out to my parents for eleven more years. When I was thirteen my family learned that I had a girlfriend and they had been less than receptive. My mother had actually set me down in front of the phone and made me call everyone in the family and out myself. She was trying to scare the gay out of me. It didn't work. In the wake of the discovery of my orientation I was too terrified to tell them the truth, that I wasn't a lesbian, I was a pansexual guy.

I went through several rough years during which I was isolated from family and friends. I was homeless twice and ended up unemployed. It was at that point in my life I decided that the military was my only option. Initially, the military was just a job, a means to feed my family. Once I got into basic training it became so much more. For the first time who and what I was didn't matter. In the civilian world so many things had outed me, and more than a few people had discriminated against me for who I was. Now that I had joined the Air Force we were all the same. People didn't pry into my personal life and foist their beliefs on me, because we all realized we had much more important things to worry about. All that mattered was the success of my team, my flight. From the very first day I was introduced to military culture I was in love. This wasn't just a job. I had finally found a family, a place where I could belong and contribute to the world in a meaningful way. I felt as that I never wanted to do anything else but this.

Basic training was one of my biggest challenges, made even harder by the fact that I had joined while "Don't Ask, Don't Tell" was in effect. Once again, I was working desperately to hide who I was from my peers. Once again, I was faced with the prospect of unemployment and homelessness because of my sexual orientation. At any moment, someone could find out about my wife or my sexuality and leadership could move to discharge me from the service. But even more frightening was that while DADT alleged to allow gays, lesbians, and bisexuals to serve as long as they remained hidden, it didn't address trans people at all. If someone discovered my gender identity, there would be no avenues for challenging my dismissal. I was forced to live a double life. At home I was Steve, and I had a loving girlfriend. At work I was Stephanie, and I told people about my boyfriend. My life became a charade for protecting my ability to serve.

I hated having to hide who I was, and I hated myself for being a liar. Integrity wasn't just a core value of the Air Force that I had come to love dearly; it was core to the value I placed on myself. I felt like a fraud. The day DADT was repealed was a huge relief to myself and my wife, but I realized something heartbreaking—even though DADT was gone, some of us in the LGBT community had been left behind. Transgender people, like me, were still not allowed to serve as their authentic selves.

Several years later my wife left me, my mother was diagnosed with cancer, and I was going through a court case against a military supervisor who had sexually harassed and mistreated me. I was at an all-time low. At that point, I decided to spend a year trying as hard as I could to live as a "normal" female. I invested in makeup, replaced all of my clothes, and started pursuing more "feminine" activities. I was unbearably miserable. I found myself on the edge of the abyss more times than I like to admit. Another hurdle was explaining to my family that, though I had been married to a woman and they had perceived me as a lesbian, I was actually pansexual. I had never cared about the gender of the person I dated, only whether I loved them or not. Even more daunting was the thought of ever having to explain that my gender identity was male. I saw myself as male, which had nothing to do with who I was attracted to; my personal identity and my sexual preferences are independent things, but I knew that would be even harder for them to understand. Finally, I made the decision to start my transition from someone who was assigned female at birth to the man I knew myself to be. My boyfriend at the time, who has since become my husband, stood by me through it all. I was still unable to make any medical progress, but I could live and dress as myself at home.

In 2015, I saw a bright light at the end of the long dark tunnel in which I had been living. We were hearing that the ban on transgender service was being studied and that it would soon be lifted. I don't have words for what that felt like. There is no proper way to describe being seen and accepted for who you truly are. I was like a wet dog left out on the rainy streets who had finally been welcomed into a warm home after years of watching all of the other dogs play in the sun.

However, there was one catch to my transition; my husband and I wanted to have children. Over the course of a year, I went through several tests to determine how my fertility would be affected by hormone treatment and whether I could stop treatment once I had started it. None of the military doctors I saw had any real answers for me.

In 2016, the universe decided for me. I found myself unexpectedly pregnant. Needless to say, my husband and I were shocked but at the same time we were overjoyed. Even though we hadn't planned to be parents right then, we wanted children regardless.

Two months later I found myself in the emergency room having a miscarriage. I remember sitting in the hospital bed after the doctor left and just sobbing. My husband couldn't be there with me as he had taken our cat to the veterinarian, and he didn't know what was happening with me. I felt completely alone. I had waited for more than a year on my transition while we had researched fertility and debated on having children, and now it felt like it had all been for nothing. I wondered if I should have just transitioned before I had ever become pregnant and if that would have spared me from some of the heartache. Instead, I knew that both having children and living as my true self were both now even further in the future.

My husband and I talked through our loss together and decided that having been so looking forward to having a child we couldn't go back. I decided to initiate my transition, seek professional guidance on safe steps to take for doing so while pregnant, and try again for a baby. Within a month we were expecting our first-born son and I was meeting with a psychologist to start my transition plan.

My leadership had known I was transgender from the first day transgender service became legal. However, that didn't mean that every coworker I had was alright with it. In fact, I had even been referred to by a military superior as "that" because they saw me more as a thing than a person.

Talks of a possible transgender ban, following tweets from the commander in chief, started when I was seven months along. This time not only was I at risk of being unemployed, but I would also be unemployed with a brand-new baby. Needless to say, I was terrified. After my son was born it was a race against time to start hormones, then to schedule my top surgery. I was able to get my surgery only days before the ban went into effect and, thankfully, I was informed that I would be grandfathered in. Even though I know my career and my family are safe for the moment, I don't feel victorious. This time I'm the one able to play in the sun, but my transgender brothers and sisters who weren't grandfathered in? They have been left outside in the rain.

Alexandria Holder, Technical Sergeant, U.S. Air Force, 2004–present

Operation Golden Flow. Operation Sausage Gaze. Meat gazing. Hydration monitor. Clam shucking. Wiz quiz. Piss test. Urinalysis.

Military folk young and old will be nodding sagely, memories of plastic cups, close quarters, and streams of urine flowing through their minds. Civilians may also have the experience of drug testing and pregnancy tests, but the military has industrialized the process in a way that would cause shivers in the non–uniformed service population.

On a chilly winter day, I walked happily into work, a spring in my step and a song on my lips. I had a number of things on my mind, but all of the things that I had to do that day were nice and simple. It was going to be a relaxed, easy Monday. Or so I thought.

After settling into my office and logging into my various computers, my unit's first sergeant popped his head into the room. He looked concerned, and a concerned first sergeant is never a good thing.

"Sergeant Holder? Do you have a moment?"

I immediately locked my machines and stood up. "Of course, sir."

Panic descended. What did I do wrong (this time)? How much trouble was I going to be in?

We entered his office, and he asked me to sit down. The door shut ominously.

"Sergeant Holder, how is your transition going?"

I was nearing the date of completion of my transition from male to female, but I hadn't yet had everything "officially" done in all the military computer systems.

"Going well, sir. I should be done in the next month or so."

"Forgive me if this is really personal, but have you had any surgeries?"

Typically asking transgender people about surgeries is very taboo, but I have encouraged people in my unit to ask me questions. I believe very strongly about educating the curious and have used my experiences as a springboard to get those around me to accept others going through transition.

"Just one, sir. I had my trachea shaved—" I pointed to my neck, "and I hadn't planned on doing anything else for the time being."

He started to look more nervous.

"You . . . uh . . . have been selected for urinalysis."

I started to giggle nervously. Oh, dear lord, a random drug test. At *this* point in my transition.

I had an exception-to-policy letter that allowed me to adhere to female dress and appearance standards, so I had long hair, makeup, and earrings. I had no facial hair, and my ancestry blessed me with naturally more feminine features. I was routinely recognized as being female, and boy, this would be an interesting adventure.

"Uhhh . . . yes, sir. It's my duty to provide a sample if required."

"Well, take your time. If you feel like you can't do this the commander and I will try to do something."

"Sir, I really appreciate it, but I wouldn't want to put you or the colonel out. I'll read the regulations and do my best."

"Just let me know. Thanks for being so understanding."

"Absolutely, sir."

I got up and returned to my office. I turned to my good old friends, the Air Force Instructions. I read guidance and policies, memorandums, and more instructions than I normally do in a month. All of them told me the same thing: the gender in Air Force computer systems was the one under which I would be tested. This lady was going to have to pee in front of a dude.

I steeled my courage and went to sign my letter stating I understood the reporting instructions for the urinalysis. I first drank a couple of cups of coffee and some water in preparation. I then walked the half mile to the urinalysis office.

I checked into the office, showed them my ID card, and told them I was ready to go. The young airman signing me in looked extremely confused. He looked at me and my ID card, all visibly female, and then at the list in front of him. Looked up. Looked down. Then he called for help from the head of the office. They discussed my case briefly, but this did nothing to relax the airman. If anything, he seemed to be more stressed.

"A . . . a uh . . . male observer, please."

Every head turned to stare at me. It was at this point that I started to feel better. I was nervous, sure. But I knew who I was. I knew what I was going through. But for everyone else this was unexplored territory. *EVERYONE THERE WAS MORE NERVOUS THAN I WAS.*

The observer moved forward. I took this moment to try to defuse the situation a bit.

"Just so you know, I'm transitioning. I still have male parts."

"Oh . . . okay," said the observer. He seemed to be relieved that he was going to be looking at a penis. "Let's get this over with."

I lifted my cup over my head, keeping it in plain view of the observer. We walked into the restroom and I washed my hands. Water only, no soap. I dried them, and then made my way over to the toilet.

"Hey, just to make things easier I'll just stay standing. Work for you?"

"Uh, yeah, that works."

I unbuttoned the front of my uniform and did my business. I filled it most of the way, then finished off in the toilet. I buttoned up with one hand, then washed, this time with soap.

We made our way back into the office and completed the administrative part of the urinalysis.

Before I left, I turned to my observer. "Hey, thanks for being so respectful." He looked relieved. "Oh, no worries. I wasn't sure what to do at first, but you were cool about it."

As I left, I had time to reflect on what I had gone through over the past couple of hours, and to see in that a reflection of my transition as a whole. I had felt fear and panic, and a heaping portion of discomfort, because of the awkwardness of my transition and the dangly bits remaining between my legs. But, at the end of the day, I did my duty, had the chance to educate some folk, and successfully passed my pee test. Nothing bad happened, and everyone was respectful and professional.

Every transition has its moments of uncertainty and strangeness: promotion to a new rank; moving to a new unit; learning a new mission; becoming a military member or retiring as a civilian. But what carries the military forward is the firm foundation of respect and professionalism that is instilled in every uniformed service member. We will always have individuals that do not adapt well to this foundation; this was seen with the desegregation of the military in 1947, the repeal of "Don't Ask, Don't Tell" in 2011, and, in 2013, the move to officially permit women to hold combat roles. Yet the military is stronger because of its diversity and openness, and there are always benefits to having people with different backgrounds and experiences serving together. And, just as there were no major issues with any of these previous decisions, the people in uniform today are more than capable of embracing transgender people openly serving, just as they have done since June of 2016.

Operation Golden Flow: successful.

Jamie Hash, Master Sergeant, U.S. Air Force, 2011–present

For as long as I can remember, I have always been a part of a team. From romping around the local recreational center with my fellow toddlers and frantically chasing a ball to serving as captain of my college soccer team and playing in the NCAA tournament, being on a soccer team taught me what it means to be a part of something bigger than myself. I grew up very competitive, constantly seeking perfection, and always trying to prove myself, especially when it came to soccer. It has only been in the last few years that I realized soccer wasn't just my primary passion for the vast majority of my life, it also served as a mechanism for allowing me to compartmentalize and internalize something that I had struggled with ever since I was that toddler. While I played on the boys' team, there was something conflicting inside me that I hadn't been able to articulate.

As my soccer career was coming to a close and I was entering adulthood, I began thinking about the next chapter in my life. I was subconsciously craving something else that would allow me to continue denying the feelings that I locked away in my internal closet. How could I continue being part of a team and something bigger than myself? How, at the same time, could I continue to challenge myself?

I grew up down the road from Marine Corps Base Quantico, many of my friends had military parents, my mother worked in Army human resources as a civilian, both of my grandfathers served in the Army, and my uncle served in the Air Force. I eventually realized that I also belonged on that team.

In my early twenties, I fully invested my time and energy to joining the Air Force, working with my recruiter to send me to basic training as soon as possible. Sitting at the Military Entrance Processing Station, I eagerly awaited this new adventure. I read through the never-ending documentation, quickly learned the culture of "hurry up and wait," and signed my name and initials what felt like over a thousand times. One of these initialed lines was signed confidently, without hesitation, in which

I agreed to the outdated terminology of never having "current or history of psychosexual conditions, including but not limited to transsexualism, exhibitionism, transvestism, voyeurism, and other paraphilias" (eye roll). At this point in my life, I had not fully confronted the feelings that I had buried deep down from a young age. I learned very early in life that contradicting society's gender norms was frowned upon by the authority figures in my life. Therefore, I denied the authentic version of myself and learned to adapt to what I believed others wanted me to be. With joining the military, I felt confident that my recently adapted hypermasculine phase would help me continue to suppress and, ultimately, conquer my true feelings.

During basic training, I held a top leadership position and, during the final ceremony, was named an honor graduate. During my aircraft armament technical training, I also held a leadership position and was named the top distinguished graduate in my class. Upon graduation, I traveled to my first duty station in Goldsboro, North Carolina, where I worked on the weapons systems of F-15E Strike Eagles, ground-attack fighter jets. Within the initial months of being with my first unit, I was nicknamed "Steve Rogers" (aka Captain America) for being a fit and driven performer. I also volunteered, went to church (in an attempt to pray away the trans), worked out religiously, and strived to be an expert at my new job. I loved the camaraderie that came with working on the flight line, and it was readily apparent that I had found my new team.

After over two years of occupational training, becoming more proficient as an aircraft armament technician, winning quarterly and annual load crew awards, and even being promoted six months early to senior airman, I was offered a position as a standard lead crew member. This was a quality assurance role charged with training and inspecting all aircraft armament technicians and munitions-loading procedures on the base. Going up to "Load Barn," as it was dubbed, as a brand-new senior airman was extremely rare. I quickly seized the opportunity and started earning multiple Airman of the Quarter and Armament Technician of the Quarter awards. I was even named the Maintenance Professional of the Year, which earned me a two-foot bronze statue. Before I was tasked for my first deployment, I made staff sergeant in my first year of eligibility, which up until that point was the pinnacle of my career.

In 2014, I joined members of my first unit in a deployment with the joint coalition against ISIS (Islamic State of Iraq and Syria) in Southwest Asia. This was at the same time that President Barack Obama declared an escalation against the extremist group, and my unit was the first F-15 unit to join that effort. As soon as my boots hit the ground, I recognized the intensity and high ops tempo. While the majority of my time was consumed by ensuring "warheads hit foreheads," as people referred to completing the mission, the down time I did have was spent working out and grappling with how I wanted to live the rest of my life. I've spoken to many people about how deployments make it feel like your life is on pause, while your friends and family are back home moving forward with their lives. Deployment can really make you focus on what is truly important in your life.

In addition to receiving a decoration for the work I did during deployment, there was something else of merit that I attained: a sense of self-acceptance. As you may have noticed, I haven't opened up much about being transgender. This is to illustrate that the recognition for my performance has nothing to do with my gender identity.

Even though I had finally accepted my truth at that time, the original ban on transgender military service was still in place. When I returned home from deployment, I had a new assignment as a manpower analyst at Joint Base San Antonio. I moved away from the East Coast for the first time in my life. This geographical separation allowed me the freedom and space to finally begin allowing those feelings I'd repressed my whole life to surface. After decades of fear and disavowing my membership in the LGBTQ+ community, I began getting involved in the San Antonio and Austin LGBTQ+ communities. Volunteering with many different organizations allowed me to meet people with similar life experiences for the first time in my life.

In 2016, about six months after arriving in Texas, I read a news article about how Defense Secretary Ash Carter had established a working group the year prior to look into the transgender military policy. While this gave me hope, I still wasn't sure I'd have the strength and courage to fully come out in my personal and professional life. In 2016, the week before San Antonio Pride, Carter announced that the ban would be lifted, and a new policy would be rolled out in the coming year. I couldn't believe that it was actually happening. There was a mixed feeling of rejoice, fear, and uncertainty.

At that point of my life, I was only out to a small group of friends. One was my new best friend and future partner, a pivotal source of support as I gradually started coming out to more friends, family, and eventually my unit. I like to think that I was very methodical in my coming out process. With every person I came out to, I had to prepare myself to potentially lose that relationship forever. The process was mentally taxing, and coming out to my unit leadership was no different. I had just been named the Non-Commissioned Officer (NCO) of the Quarter for my entire field operating agency, so that had to help, right? In every situation in my life, I expect the worse and hope for the best. I don't think I could've hoped for better support than what I received from my unit leadership.

I will never forget my commander's words when we had our meeting. He said, "While this is a big deal for you, this is not a big deal for the squadron. You are still the same NCO who just won a quarterly award, and you are still the same high performer." After the Department of Defense policy was implemented, the Air Force followed suit and required that every unit provide a one-time, face-to-face transgender awareness training. My commander went on to allow me to facilitate the training so that I could share my story and address potential misconceptions. As my story spread throughout Joint Base San Antonio, I was given other speaking opportunities where I was able to spread awareness and educate numerous military organizations.

I couldn't have asked for a more supportive environment to undergo my journey towards living authentically. During this journey, I found another team—SPARTA. SPARTA is a group, existing largely through social media, consisting of nearly a thousand transgender service members in the U.S. military, enabling those of any rank and serving all over the world to connect for support and resources. As military members, we aren't able to choose where we live, and sometimes our duty stations are in austere locations without any LGBTQ+ presence. In situations like these, SPARTA becomes integral for support and community.

It seemed like everything was starting to fall into place in my life, but in the summer of 2017, I learned via Twitter that I would no longer be able "to serve in any capacity." With six years of service, perfect performance ratings, numerous accolades, and multiple medals, my service was all of sudden in question because of my gender identity. During the year, with the new ban put on hold by four federal injunctions, I was promoted to technical sergeant in my first year of eligibility, named the Non-Commissioned Officer of the Year for my field operating agency, received the Joint Base San Antonio military volunteer of the year award, and I was nominated for the Force Support Non-Commissioned Officer of the Year and the 12 Outstanding Airmen of the Year Award. I also recently completed my master of science degree in organizational performance improvement with a 4.0 GPA, which I started around the same time I began coming out. I always try to allow my performance to speak for itself, and, being transgender, my accomplishments mean even more since my service is now under such high scrutiny.

I never intended on being an outspoken transgender military member or being forced to defend my ability to serve. Once the transgender military ban became a national story, I was contacted by numerous media outlets for interviews, and I leveraged those platforms to advocate for transgender military service. People, some of whom I had never met before, began approaching me and telling me that I changed their perspective on transgender military service and trans people in general. My partner, the creator of the LGBTQ+ blog *Profiles in Pride*, always tells people that stories are the most powerful weapon we have to change hearts and minds. I now try to engage that weapon as often as I can. Now that the ban has officially been implemented, I feel extremely fortunate being able to serve under the exemption clause since I transitioned before the new policy's cutoff date. Throughout history, there have always been marginalized groups of people that had to fight for equality in the military, but the military's policies have always been a driver of social change. Whether it was desegregation, women in combat, or the repeal of "Don't Ask, Don't Tell" permitting LGB people to serve openly, the military's policies have ultimately sent ripples throughout the rest of society. This is just the next frontier.

Ever since July 2017, though, there has been a looming cloud of uncertainty regarding my future with the U.S. Air Force. Serving openly and authentically has allowed me to be a better performer, a better wingman, and the best version of myself. I have been a member of many teams throughout my life, but right now, my team is a finite group of resilient transgender military service members who have the responsibility of proving that transgender troops are fully capable of serving honorably and serving for those who cannot.

Tyler "Billy" Billiet, Technical Sergeant, U.S. Air Force, 2013–present

On August 27, 2013, I enlisted in the United States Air Force as a female and headed to boot camp. In June 2016, transgender persons were told we could serve openly in the United States military. Thirteen months later, in July 2017, transgender persons were told we could not serve in the United States military. In December 2017, I ended my service as a female in the Air Force and began serving as a male. As I write this in July 2019, I am recovered from my most recent transition-related procedure. I had surgery at a Naval Medical Center a few months ago and it was a great experience filled with military medical professionals who treated me with nothing but respect and care. They were happy for me, asked me questions about my transition, and treated me like any other patient and brother-in-arms. This positivity has resonated throughout my experience as a transgender service member; for that, I am thankful. That is my motivation for sharing my story.

2011

Alicante, Spain: One text message during a semester abroad changed my life forever. While I spent the first five months of 2011 studying in Spain, my roommates back in Minnesota had realized something about me that I had not yet picked up on: I was transgender. Seems they watched a documentary about transgender individuals and thought of me. I immediately jumped on Google and spent the next few hours researching anything and everything related to being transgender. By the end of the night, I realized that my roommates had picked up on something in these peoples' lives that paralleled something in mine and brought it to light. This is what I have been feeling? How did I not know?! Turns out that is not uncommon; I googled that as well.

2012

My senior year of college consisted of me obsessing over my gender and this new revelation, dating a girl for the first time and subsequently being viewed and labeled (albeit not self-proclaimed) as a lesbian, and truly realizing how confusingly intertwined gender and sexuality really could be. I began to speak with military recruiters, exploring various ways to serve. Cliché as it might sound, I had wanted to join the military since I was a little kid; my cousins and I spent hours playing "Army," going on missions across my yard, their yard, and Grandma and Grandpa's yard, sometimes admiring and trying on my uncle's battle dress uniform (BDU), the green camouflage uniform with which many are familiar.

As a political science student, I was aware of the repeal of "Don't Ask, Don't Tell" in 2011 and what that meant for the L, G, and B service members, but I was not sure what that meant for the T service members. Once again, I had to turn to Google for some very important life advice: "Are transgender people allowed to join the U.S. military?" No, no they are not, not openly anyway. I remember thinking and debating with myself, "It's okay, I'll do my four years and then I can separate and transition" or "If I love the military, which I probably will, I'll do my twenty years and just forget about this gender stuff until later in life . . . I can do that, right? It's only a few years . . . couple decades . . . ."

2013

After reading about trans military personnel, I didn't dare ask my recruiters if Google was correct, nor did I dare mention anything about being LGBT. While I was completely uncomfortable being seen as a woman in men's apparel and thus assumed to be gay, I knew that assumption was better than the truth in this situation.

After graduation, I applied to Air Force Officer Training School, but when I wasn't selected, I enlisted instead. I was about to attend boot camp, put on a uniform each day, and serve my country. Every visit to the Military Entrance Processing Station (MEPS) made me more and more excited for this new adventure, although still a little bit nervous. Little did I truly understand how much of my nervousness was attributed to my gender. I knew I could keep up with at least some of the guys—I had a black belt in Tae Kwon Do and had run competitively for the last decade. That was not the issue. The issue, I learned with hindsight, was the anxiety and dysphoria that my assigned gender caused.

2014

Basic training was two of the most awesome months of my life. Hardly any time at all was devoted to thinking about anything other than the military, food, or sleep. Tech school (job training) was almost as awesome. Almost. One day the gender thing, in all its terrible and glorious pink and blue fashion, came barreling back into my life. I cried to my class leader, Katie, and indirectly told her about these feelings that were resurfacing. I was careful to sidestep the issue and avoid saying "transgender"—that would make it too real and scary to mention at the time. If she figured it out during the conversation she never mentioned it. Today Katie and her wife, Nicole, remain two of the most important people in my life.

I pushed those thoughts to the back of my mind as best as I could as I made my way to my first duty station, Beale Air Force Base in Northern California. I focused on learning my job, exploring California with friends, and being a normal twenty-four-year-old in the military. The only problem was that everything, literally everything, would force the dysphoria and this gender thing to the forefront of my brain. I was expending so much energy obsessing over my gender, how it impacted my life, and whether or not I wanted to transition, that I was always exhausted.

I was missing out on life. I passed up opportunities to hang out with friends and have fun because I was uncomfortable doing various activities as a female. I was continually saddened by that. My dating life and relationships were plagued with issues that were really only masking this gigantic, yet silent, issue. How could I be happy with or love somebody else if I was unhappy and could not love myself? I started realizing I could not live like this forever. Doing my time in the military and ignoring this was going to be impossible. I needed to find help, I needed to sort through this, I needed to *live*.

2015

I identified local nonprofits that offered counseling programs, support/ social groups, and hormone clinics. I started paying out of pocket for counseling and travel costs just so that I could talk to someone. I was putting a couple hundred miles on my car each week to attend group therapy so to not feel alone, to figure out my life. I was scared, I was nervous, and I was doing all of this in secret, not even telling my friends why I was gone one or two evenings every single week. I also was not ready to tell my family. I was almost positive I was trans, but admitting it would make it real. Being more sure of myself, however, made it harder to ignore my truth and sit in the closet while dysphoria banged on the door behind which my career stood.

The dysphoria continued to be a constant and consuming buzz that kept me in a gray fog. This haze would not lift no matter what, not for any length of time. My mirror was covered in Christmas wrapping paper because otherwise I could not get dressed and leave my room. The only moments of peace came to me as I slept. I wanted to sleep forever because that was the only time I found any peace and quiet within. I did not want to exist as I was and with how I felt. I do not think I actually wanted to die; I just did not want to live. I wished I had been born the person I knew myself to be so that I would not have to go through this turmoil. This scared the shit out of me. I finally realized what sleeping forever meant, what not wanting to live meant. I knew I had to fight because I wanted to know how my story was to turn out.

In 2015 the military entered a "gray area" for its transgender members in that we would not be automatically discharged while the policy was reviewed. Any such decision would not be in the hands of one's local command but would be elevated to a high level. I printed off that policy memo and carried it around with me every day as I started to tell trusted colleagues. I remember admitting to my friend Angie, who at the time was in my chain of command, why I could not make up my mind about what I wanted to do with my career. I was not just being indecisive or picky or becoming complacent because there was a lot more at stake. She was supportive from that moment on, encouraging me to go to group, to do what makes me happy, assuring me that everything would fall into place.

2016

If I had only twenty-four hours to say either yes or no to hormones and would never have the opportunity again, would I do it? This was the question I asked myself when I was unsure I was embarking on the correct journey. Of course I would. With that, I knew I had to medically transition. The incessant noise that is dysphoria was not going to subside without transitioning. Taking advantage of the "gray area" the military was in with regard to trans service members, I made an appointment with a civilian hormone clinic. To my dismay I found there was a three-month wait. I used those three months to muster all the courage it was going to take to start coming out to my military medical provider and my leadership. If I was going to do this, I was going to do it as correctly as possible, I was going be the right kind of example of a transgender airman.

I was so nervous that I thought for sure I was going to puke on many important people's floors. The women's health provider was the first person I told, and she was so excited for me to start this journey! Whew, what a relief! My voice was shaking and I wanted to cry, first because of nerves and then because of happiness. I then had to tell the family physician, who was my assigned doctor, so that I could have the proper paperwork in place as I started hormones. She hugged me. Of course, the paperwork needed to be signed by my commander via my first sergeant. I was beyond nervous to meet with my first sergeant, Eric, and come out to him. I have a lot of respect for that man and the stripes he wears and I did not want to disappoint him. Angie set up a meeting time with him and she came with me. Every word that came out of his mouth after I managed to shakily tell him that I am transgender and am about to start transitioning was full of respect, care, and pride. He stepped into the commander's office and motioned me in once the lieutenant colonel said he had a free moment—so I could come out all over again. Once again, I had words of encouragement and support from allies embarking on this journey with me.

In June, I watched the video stream of Secretary of Defense Ash Carter announce the repeal of the ban on transgender service members. Shaking and holding back tears of joy, I rushed to the intelligence section of base to go talk to Eric, my first sergeant. I had my paperwork from the clinic awaiting my commander's signature. The timing could not have been any better! When I found that Eric was not in his office I figured I would search for Angie on the operations floor and tell her the good news. I had dreamt of my reaction to this news for months—where I would be, how I would respond, etc. The news, my reaction, and the support I received that day was so much better than I ever imagined! I could not find Angie, but I just about ran right into my friend Christina and emotionally told her about Secretary Carter's announcement. We finally found Angie in an office and motioned her out. I am sure she could see something was up. Through sobs and a waterfall of happy tears I managed to choke out the announcement that Secretary Carter made, saying over and over "I get to be myself!" I have never cried so hard from happiness. We all ended up sitting on the floor crying while passersby asked what was going on and if everything was okay. Little did they know everything was more than okay. I was going to be able to *live my life* and keep my beloved career.

I received my first shot of testosterone on September 4, 2016, and I knew right away I would never look back. The next morning, I woke up with a clear mind for the first time in my whole life. I liken this experience to that of a cloudy, gray day that all of a sudden breaks, leaving the sun shining brightly against blue skies.

2017

This was a year of ups and downs. The Department of Defense and each branch's policy regarding in-service gender transition were slightly different and brand-new, which factored into having top surgery both scheduled and canceled, as well as a half-year-long grueling battle for an exception to policy so that I could wear male uniforms. I was afforded a bit of a fresh start at Airman Leadership School (which is why I so badly wanted to be able to wear male uniforms) during which "the tweets" happened, I finally had top surgery, and I changed my gender marker. I also spent a year outside of my Air Force Specialty Code (AFSC = job) serving as the Base Honor Guard Assistant Non-Commissioned Officer in Charge; it was such an awesome and humbling opportunity. Not only was I working with mostly people who did not know me from Adam but serving in the Honor Guard is highly visible to the local communities. I truly was just another guy in the Air Force. Thankfully, through all the ups and downs I continued to have supportive leadership by my side. My future was bright, so incredibly bright.

2018

The last couple of years have been both hectic and on cruise control at the same time. I have been readjusting back to my intelligence AFSC position and becoming a team lead, leading eight airmen in mission execution every day, as well as still trudging through the process of transitioning while in the military, pursuing subsequent surgeries strategically so I can have the least amount of hiccups in my career and mitigating my time away from work. At times, the process feels painstakingly slow, putting my career on pause while I bring my body and mind together as one. I know that the conclusion of my transition is in the near future and I will finally be able to confidently and comfortably pursue a commission and career field change. I am five courses away from finishing a master's degree and a handful of months away from wearing E-6, technical sergeant. I could not have gotten this far without the trust and support of my coworkers and leadership every step of the way. I doubt any of them will ever truly understand the struggle involved, as I very intentionally put on a smile, maintain a positive attitude, and carry myself in a way that it does not show. I am not afraid of showing hardship and vulnerability, but I am a true believer in leading my airmen in a manner in which they do not realize I am simultaneously undergoing this amazing transition. Doing so not only educates those around me but will help foster an environment of support for the transgender airmen who will follow in my footsteps.

Sabrina Bruce, Technical Sergeant, U.S. Air Force/Space Force, 2013–present

Integrity first. We learn these words in our first week of basic training. In addition to "service before self" and "excellence in all we do," they make up the three Air Force core values. But integrity always comes first. Without integrity, the other two are meaningless. When I first yelled those words, on a dark October morning in San Antonio, I had no idea how they would come to define my life. Integrity isn't a day-to-day thing; it is a lifestyle. I came to grips with that fact as I struggled to live life as a male. How could I go each day pretending to be something I'm not?

The definition of integrity is "the state of being whole and undivided." For twenty-six years I lived a divided life, hopelessly wishing to be something else, to have been born a woman and be happy in my own skin. I was living a life that never quite fit, despite how hard I tried. My motto was "Fake it till you make it." I was good at faking, but never made it. Tediously, I moved further along in my twenties, doing my best to ignore the yearning in my soul, that desire to live a life on the outside that reflected how I felt on the inside. As I had nothing better to do, I attended college and quickly fell into the party scene, trying to find myself among others. Mindlessly, I worked towards a degree that I had no passion for, attended classes with no motivation to succeed, and dreaded going out into the real world. My apathy towards school was reflected in my grades; many mornings I couldn't summon the will to even get out of bed and attend—I'm surprised I didn't fail more classes than I did. Finally, in 2012, I gave up completely on school and began drifting between work, home, and whatever friend's house that had alcohol. I promised my parents I would go back, that I just needed a break. Every night, I would go to bed, wishing I could be better, that I could summon the will to care about my life again. Sadly, life isn't a fairy tale and wishes don't come true unless you put in the effort to make them true.

The summer of 2012 is one I hardly remember; my days were spent sleeping and my nights were spent doing my best to forget the mess I had made of my life. Finally, the shock I needed happened. Some of my friends got into trouble with the police and I found myself mired in a bad situation. Seeing them get in trouble and have their lives ruined showed me that I needed to do something, anything to get my life back in order. In October of 2012, I found myself in an Air Force recruiting office, my last, best option to turn things around. Being a child of the War on Terror, I had grown up with the military being a constant presence in the house. My parents held the military in high regard, approaching soldiers to shake their hands, thanking them for their service; they always seemed proud of other sons who had gone off to do their part for the country. I wanted that, to have something to make my parents proud, something to give me direction and discipline in life, something to hopefully make me a man.

Basic training came and went. Life is simple but busy those first few months after you go away to basic. You lose yourself in the routine and keep your mind either too busy or too tired to worry about much. For the first time in a long time, I had something that resembled peace in my life. Inside that peace, I began to finally feel like I had somewhere I could belong and fit in. Each month I wore the uniform, I found that my confidence steadily rose. It no longer felt I was just "faking" it, but that I was finally "making" it. I became an exemplary airman; no task was too big for me. But the peace was not built to last, the plaster I had covered over the cracks slowly fell apart. Integrity is first because it is essential to doing things right. We may hide a flaw or a problem for a long time, almost forgetting it is there. But it's never gone forever, and when that problem comes back, it usually comes back with a vengeance.

In the fall of 2014, I made my first tentative steps towards accepting myself. I told my best friend that I liked to cross-dress and, to my astonishment, she wasn't repulsed or horrified; she simply shrugged her shoulders and reassured me that it was fine. That small act of acceptance blossomed a seed of hope in my heart that maybe I could live as a woman and not have the world come crashing down. Halloween that year, I went out dressed as a woman. It was liberating to go out as a woman, and it all just felt so right. But that was only one night. Many other nights I fought against my desire to transition and would tell myself that I just have a feminine side that I need to express occasionally. I would look in the mirror and count the flaws in my body, the masculine features that would stand out were I ever to transition. My jaw was too strong, my shoulders too big, my forehead too high. I found a hundred different excuses to not accept who I was. I knew I was lying to myself, but when you live a lie so long, when you hide in that darkness, you become afraid of ever stepping out into the light.

In early 2016, rumors began to circulate about the ban on transgender service members being lifted. The thing I had run from for so long might actually be something I could pursue in the Air Force. This scared me. Again I found myself in the mirror, looking at myself with butterflies in my stomach as I imagined living life as a woman.

All I could see was my little life being flipped upside down, the stability and respect I had worked so hard to earn thrown out. My family, who was so proud of me, would turn their backs on me. Ban or no ban, coming out as transgender would expose a part of me that I had worked so hard to conceal.

The summer of 2016 came and I found myself deployed to Djibouti, Africa. The ban was lifted, but I was far removed from any news and I was too busy at work to really think about it. But one night, as I worked my shift, a coworker came across an article about Logan Ireland. He mentioned it off hand in the shop and my ears perked up. I rushed to find it and read it for myself. My heart was racing as I began to read about a man who had taken that leap. Logan's life wasn't ruined; in fact, he seemed happy. He was living his life truthfully, with integrity. He had taken that step, looking dysphoria in the face and saying, "not one more day." He had made himself whole, and if he could do it, why couldn't I?

After reading that article, my thoughts again began to swirl. Was I strong enough to take that leap? Thinking back on my life up till that point, how many things had I done that once seemed insurmountable? Before I went to basic training, I didn't think I could make it through, that I wasn't tough enough to succeed, but I had. I hadn't thought I was smart enough to finish my technical training but I did, with some of the highest grades in the class. When I tested for staff sergeant, I walked out thinking I would never make it but when the results were posted three months later, I was the number one select in my career field. Little by little, the Air Force handed me challenges and showed me that I could overcome them.

My gender dysphoria seemed so much greater; it had been a monster in my life, poisoning everything I had done, constantly whispering into my ear that I was wrong, that I was broken, that I was perverted. Could I finally face that monster instead of constantly running from it? I spent many nights drifting through camp, looking up to the stars for answers, but only darkness answered back. I struggled with acceptance for months, my walls slowly crumbling. It was a painful process; I spent many days laying in my bed, not wanting to get out as I felt my world was falling down around me. Mindlessly I went to work, feeling off and not at all like the person I used to be. My coworkers didn't know me well enough to realize that something was wrong. At points, I wanted to scream to them, "This isn't me, I'm not like this, I don't think I'm okay!" My night began to darken, but it is always darkest right before the dawn.

A new year began on January 1, 2017. My new life began thirteen days later when I finally accepted who I was. I sat in my work center, having a small, silent breakdown as I spoke with my best friend over instant messenger. She knew about my struggle, having given me that hope two years prior when I confessed my cross-dressing to her. But even she didn't know how it had consumed me for the past few months. I typed the words out, that I wanted to live life as a woman, coming to work, going out, everything. After I sent that message, I knew my mind was made up—I would do my best to live life the way I was meant to. I arrived back to America a few weeks later, feeling blessed that my time in Africa was over. A few weeks later, I had made my appointment with mental health and began the long process of finally facing down that monster instead of running from it.

From that moment on, I began living my best life. Little by little I built myself back up, putting the pieces back together of my broken house. My squadron in Colorado was the rock that I stood upon as I worked to make these great changes in my life. Throughout 2017, I embraced the Air Force again, feeling that same sense of belonging I had once held. Finally I was living my life truthfully and it showed, as I once again began to excel, buoyed with self-confidence. Each day, each week I progressed in accepting myself. I couldn't go to work yet presenting as female, but when I was not on duty, I lived life as a woman. It was hard to do at times; some days I would be afraid to leave my house, afraid I would be ridiculed or hurt. But a life lived in fear is no life at all. Throughout this period, I was constantly reassured by my peers, by my supervisor, by my commander and leadership team. As I discussed my transition with them, they never laughed at me or thought I was joking; they simply listened and gave me their support. All those years when thinking about transitioning I had expected to be ridiculed, made fun of, abandoned, or beaten up. None of those fears I had turned out to be as big as I had made them out to be. Lies have a way of becoming bigger the longer we live them; at a point coming clean and telling the truth seems like suicide. In the end, though, honesty trumps lies and is never as hard as it seems.

Abraham Lincoln once said, "A house divided against itself cannot stand." In my experience, I have found that to be true for people as well. We can only live so long fighting against ourselves. When I first heard "Integrity first," I thought it was about not lying and being honest. But as I've grown, I've found that it means more than that—it's about courage, the courage to accept who you are and to do your best to be a damned good person in a world that isn't always easy. Being transgender is at its heart about integrity. The world tells transgender people that we are born a certain way and you live with it. If you feel that you are the wrong gender then you must be confused or lying to yourself. But the real lie comes from the world, the lie that the people around us know our hearts better than we do. Our integrity never allows us to peacefully accept a life lived in the wrong gender, because we know it's fake, that it is wrong, and that we aren't living truthfully to ourselves. Because in our hearts, we know how we are and who we are meant to be. We know it so strongly that sometimes it seems impossible to live life any other way.

My acceptance of myself as transgender was a culmination of work I didn't even realize I was doing. Every seemingly misguided step was a part of the path that led me to the proper place where I could realize my potential and grow into who I was meant to be. Joining the Air Force, learning about its history, it's tenets, its core values were a culmination of this journey. Without even knowing it, the Air Force was shaping me to have the courage to accept myself, to overcome a challenge that had seemed so daunting. Perhaps my life would have been easier if I weren't born transgender, but I know I would not be half the woman I am today without the strength I learned from my struggles.

Sterling J. Crutcher, Senior Airman, U.S. Air Force, 2015–present

I joined the United States Air Force in 2015, leaving for basic training in August and arriving at my first duty station in December. During this time, I knew that the Obama administration was exploring lifting the trans ban, but that it wasn't going to happen without a fight. I knew a few of the people involved in that fight and had it on good authority that it was going to be lifted and that it would be safe for me to enlist. I came out in 2016, after the ban had been lifted.

There was a lot of confusion from my chain of command. The change had just been announced and it was going to be a while before policy was set out for each branch. But, critically, my chain of command gave me their full support. They were willing to work with me to try to figure out the steps that we needed to take to make everything okay. They were respectful of my pronouns and, even though they didn't have to do so at the time, they made sure that there was no harassment from NCOs, peers, or from anyone I worked with because they didn't want volatile attitudes going around. They remained supportive of me and made sure that I was okay, making sure that I wasn't being mistreated in any way, which I wasn't. Those that disagreed with the lifting of a ban kind of kept their opinions away from me, which was good.

I had started hormones with a civilian provider in February of 2016. I had turned all that paperwork into the military before officially coming out. They knew I was on hormones, but there was no official reason why. Those assigned female at birth are often prescribed hormones for reasons unrelated to gender transition. So it wasn't an issue that I had done so. Then, in July 2017, the tweets about banning transgender people from the military came out.

That was a huge, huge bummer. It definitely put a lot of stress on everyone's shoulders. Again, my command was super supportive, all the way up to the wing level. And at that time, with the support of my command, I had done a few different interviews about what was going on. My commander actually assigned me my own personal public affairs specialist (PAS) just to make sure that I knew what to say and how to say it, as well as what not to say. Basically, it was just to help not get myself or anyone else in trouble. The PAS was fantastic and super supportive. Essentially, he would talk to any news crew before we actually did the sit-down interview so they knew, "Hey, don't cross these lines here. Don't say stuff like this." This was all to ensure that we stayed within the Air Force standards for speaking to the media. My biggest takeaway from all of that is just how supportive the military was, because I don't have a lot of support within my family or even a lot of the people with whom I grew up.

My immediate family does not support who I am, so to have that support in my chain of command, from my spouse, and from the friends that I have in the military was a huge game changer. Without that support, I don't know that I would have survived all of the pressure. It's a lot to handle if you're already dealing with the "regular" stressors of military life and don't have anyone else in your life to fall back on, to talk to, with whom to just feel like a human being. It's a lot of stress on you mentally and physically. Receiving that support from my spouse and my command over and over again has been one of the most uplifting experiences. It gave me great courage to just continue pushing forward, even when things don't seem like they're going to pan out for us. It's great to know that we're not alone.

I've had three different squadron commanders and at this point three different wing commanders and, when they find out that they have a transgender troop, every last one of them has been supportive. My current commander, a colonel, actually reached out to me. It's very uncommon for a wing commander to just email an airman, but he shot me an email one day, just expressing his support and thanking me for my service, for my professionalism with the interviews. He said, "Thank you for being professional and making us all look good." That blew me away. That's not common, they don't just sit there and email airmen. They don't have time for that. He took the time to sit down, write an email out himself, sending it to me just to make sure that I was doing all right and to just let me know that in his own way, "Hey, I got your back. Thank you for having ours." I haven't ever met this man in person and I probably never will, but his small act blew my mind.

I've also had major support from my mental health provider. He's taken care of my transition since day one. For the past three and a half years, he has fought for me. He charged hard against the new policy being put in place. He straight-up told others "no" to certain things. He said, "I'm not putting my airman through that. That's not happening." He'd say things like, "That's going to impact his career negatively. I'm not going to do it." He's put himself on the line, and not only for me but for the other trans military members on base too. He put his neck out there, for the betterment of our careers, for the betterment of our transitions and our care. Having that constant support, having someone who's fighting for you has been so important. Even though they have rules to follow, they're still pointing out the flaws.

One example is that, in the Air Force, trans people have to go through a "fake" Medical Evaluation Board (MEB) to determine if someone is deployable. By "fake," I mean that one has to go through the process even though everyone knows that there are alternatives that would allow you to remain eligible for deployment—and that should be easily identified prior to being reviewed. For example, if you're on injectables, which include some versions of hormone replacement therapies, there are certain places you're not allowed to deploy. My care provider can switch me from the injectable to something else for the deployment, making it a nonissue. However, what has happened is that we've had trans military members pushed through to a "real" MEB. Then they conclude, "Oh, well, this person can't deploy. They're not going to be much use in the military." They push you through to the board, instead of just dealing with any concerns, which puts our careers at risk and basically we have to fight just to remain in service.

As far as I know, no one's been separated on this basis yet, but I know they're dealing with it. Given that an MEB process is a medical separation from the military, nothing happens overnight. Even Air Force materials will tell you that they can take years. What makes being boarded a problem is the fact that it's even in process, even if it's over and you're retained. Someone can look at your record and wonder, "Why did they MEB you? Oh, here's why. You're C2 (an assignment limitation code) coded? That might be kind of a risk for us." The limitation code will tell them someone raised the issue of whether or not you were combat or deployment ready. You end up being viewed as more of a risk, and that can affect how you're perceived in terms of retention eligibility or your ability to change career fields. Even though trans people have been shown to be as ready as any other qualified individual, some still see us as risks. So even going before a "fake" MEB can cause issues in the future.

For these reasons, my care provider has avoided getting any of us C2 coded. Even though our records show that we're on hormones, we haven't been "highlighted" because he's said, paraphrased, "I'm not going to do it because I'm not going to mess with their careers." Even in 2016, when the ban was not in place, his feeling was that this was going to come back and bite us in the ass. He simply said that he wasn't going to allow that to happen. Now, with the ban in place, it *has* come back around to—potentially—bite us.

A lot of the issues around transgender service have come from people not having the facts. I think it's important to separate one's politics from the facts. A large majority of what I'll call "negative opinions" are simply not backed up by the facts. What I would hope really reaches people is realizing that your opinion and your ideas that you hold may not actually translate to the facts that are being put in front of you. So many people just tend to look at the label of who is making a particular statement. Is that person a liberal or conservative? It's as though many of the people who oppose trans military service say, "If they're liberal, I'm not going to believe a word they say because they're just lying" or "If they're conservative, I'm more than likely to believe what they say because they pretty much believe what I believe." People need to start looking beyond labels. It's so easy for people just to throw labels out there and just call each other names based on the fact that, "Oh, you're a liberal. Oh, you're a Democrat. I'm going to call you this name because you must be a snowflake. Ha ha ha." Or, "You're conservative. You must be a hypocritical Christian. Ha ha ha." It's so prevalent in our society to look at a label and allow that label to just to be our answer, instead of looking beyond the label.

When I first read the tweets, I was one of the few that took to Facebook and made a post which went mini-viral. I received a lot of comments on it; some supportive, some not. I remember people were like, "Well, if you would just read the facts yourself, maybe you could go get help and all this stuff." When I would respond to people, I tried to ensure I had the facts lined up and understand every study and ensure that it was legit and not biased. I found a lot of the times when I would share these studies, some people would just straight-up say, "I'm not going to read that. That's from some liberal source." Even though I would say a good majority of the things that I shared with them were not from liberal sources or conservative sources, but from places like think tanks, research institutes.

I found that because I was presenting the argument, they automatically assumed that it was just from some liberal source instead of actually reading the material or even looking into the source. I found myself thinking, "Did you actually read it?" They would write, "Well I'm not going to read it because that's just some liberal bullshit, blah, blah blah." I'd think, "Okay, well you didn't actually read it and, no, it's not liberal at all. It's actually very middle of the ground." But that was one of the issues that I've recognized as being one of the core problems with everything going on—the fact that no one can seem to look beyond a stupid label. I hate labels.

I even hate being labeled trans because it's an "identifier" of who I am. But it actually tells you nothing about who I am. It tells you a very small part. Being in the military, though I am labeled a transgender troop, they recognize me for more than that. In the Air Force, we have three core values: integrity first, service before self, and excellence in all you do. I try every day to exemplify these core values. Am I perfect? No. But my command recognizes the hard work I put in and they see me as a competent well-trusted airman, not just a transgender troop. Being recognized as another airman is really the only thing I wanted. At the end of the day, I'm just another airman doing his best alongside the rest of my peers.

4

Serving with Integrity

All my military commanders, most of the people that I was involved with in the military, it didn't matter. It didn't matter that I'm transitioning. It didn't matter. All that mattered was that I was a senior non-commissioned officer, and I could do my job.
—Master Sergeant Erika W. Stoltz

Sebastian Nemec, Sergeant, U.S. Army National Guard, 2011–present

After a winter storm ripped through southern Minnesota in April 2019, the Minnesota Army National Guard was activated by Governor Tim Walz, who had just begun his term that January. I had the opportunity to accompany Governor Walz as he and Minnesota National Guard (MNNG) leadership flew to Austin, Minnesota, to learn more about the damage from the storm. A Minnesota National Guard veteran himself, Walz has been an outspoken supporter of transgender individuals serving in the United States military. On January 23, 2019, a video was published on his Twitter account, the text of which read: "The President's ban on our transgender brothers and sisters in the military is not only wrong, but weakens our national security. As Commander-in-Chief [of Minnesota's National Guard], I will do everything in my power to make sure that anyone who is willing and able to serve, can."

I am a trans man serving in the Minnesota National Guard as well as a veteran of Operation Enduring Freedom-Kuwait. In November 2011, I enlisted when I was seventeen years old and still a senior in high school. I joined the Army because I wanted to experience life in the military and I thought it would look good on a resume. The education benefits were just a bonus. When I enlisted, I didn't realize that I was transgender. I served as a female through initial entry training and during my first deployment.

In 2013, while attending college, I came to realize that I was transgender. I pursued my undergraduate degree on a university campus while being a part-time soldier. I was heavily involved with the LGBT group on campus. I was able to be open with my friends, most of whom identified as LGBT. I began experimenting with my gender expression through clothing and started to wear more masculine clothes. When I asked them to use different pronouns, my friends were very supportive. When I was at drill, I still went by "she" and "her," but it wasn't a big deal. It was just for a few days of the month.

As I was figuring out my gender identity, I was preparing to go to Maryland for a military school with a eleven-month deployment to follow. In January of 2014, I traveled to Fort Meade, Maryland, to become qualified in a new military occupational specialty (MOS). Soon afterward, in June of 2014, I was mobilized with my unit to Texas for our final training events to deploy to Kuwait. By August, we were in the desert heat.

After I returned from my deployment in April of 2015, I started my transition. I began hormone replacement therapy and the process to legally change my name and gender marker. Then I told my family and my first-line leader at my unit about my transition. The support I received from my immediate supervisor, a first lieutenant—with whom I had just served and grown to trust during an eleven-month deployment—set the standard for how all leaders should react when a soldier comes out to them as trans. The first thing she said was, "How can I help?" This was in October 2015, after then Secretary of Defense Ash Carter said service members could not be kicked out of the military based solely on being transgender, but before June 2016 when it was announced that trans personnel could serve openly.

As a member of the National Guard, I obtained medical care primarily outside of the military. I had health insurance through my university because they would cover my transition-related medical expenses, while Tricare (the military, and much more affordable, option) did not. I went ahead and pursued hormone replacement therapy and what is referred to as "top surgery," in my case, a double mastectomy with chest masculinization.

Through all of this, I didn't have many issues with my unit. In fact, I felt actively supported. My commander, first sergeant, and the full-time staff worked to make lodging accommodations whenever necessary and worked to use the pronouns "he" and "him," even though regulation did not require that they do so.

In November 2015, I had my name legally changed, updating my personnel records immediately. But updates to the government systems sometimes take a while to reach all of the related systems. In July 2016, I went to obtain a temporary profile (like a doctor's note with restrictions) after my top surgery because I couldn't lift a certain amount of weight and my movements were restricted. I remember my interaction with the medical NCO who printed out the profile for me. I hadn't had much interaction with him in the past, but we knew "of" each other. My new name was showing on his screen, but when he printed the document it contained my birth name. He tried so hard to correct it and repeatedly apologized, but he didn't have a way to fix it. The fact that it was printing with my birth name wasn't a big deal to me, but his persistence and apologies showed me that he cared and supported me. That meant so much more to me than the form being correct.

In October 2016, I had the opportunity to present the military category nominees at the Upper Midwest Chapter of the National Academy of Television, commonly known as the Midwest Emmys. This is a black-tie event attended by media organizations from across the Midwest. The presenter of this category would normally attend the event in military dress uniform. My supervisors worked some connections to help me obtain a male Army Service Uniform for the occasion. The only issue was that, technically, I was not permitted to wear the male uniform at that time. Yet since my transition my female uniform no longer fit and would have looked very out of place on me. As an attempt to remedy this, my officer told me to go to the troop medical center on base to see about getting a military diagnosis of gender dysphoria in order to obtain an exception-to-policy memorandum to allow me to wear the male uniform. This did not go well.

Back at my unit, an individual did not agree with this and wanted to reprimand me. My supervisor held her ground and supported me. This fiasco resulted in my transferring units the very next month, fortunately to a much more supportive environment. That unit is where I've felt the most at home in the military that I ever have.

In November 2015, I had legally changed my name and gender marker, including updating both my birth certificate and passport. I was able to change my name in the military right after, but the gender marker would have to wait until the new policy was released. After the new, trans-inclusive policy was released and I got my administrative packet completed, my gender marker was officially changed within the military in February 2019. My packet took longer because I needed updated paperwork from civilian medical providers since mine were older because I transitioned before the new policy was enacted. I also had to ensure I was prepared to meet the male physical fitness standards.

As of July 2019, I work full-time as a public affairs specialist for the Minnesota National Guard. As a public affairs specialist, I often work with the adjutant general of our state, Major General Jon Jensen. In the summer of 2017, I and another transgender soldier had been interviewed by a local TV news station. Also in this segment was Jensen. He expressed his support for transgender soldiers. Since then, I've worked with General Jensen enough times that, among the more than thirteen thousand soldiers and airmen he leads, he recognizes who I am. This brings me to the UH-60 Blackhawk helicopter flight that I took with him and the governor to Austin, Minnesota, in April 2019.

As I was following Jensen and the senior enlisted advisor into a gymnasium to photograph them talking with soldiers, Jensen pulled me aside. This was April 13, the day after President Trump's ban on transgender individuals serving in the U.S. military went into effect.

Jensen said that he wanted to introduce me to the governor to help put a face to transgender people serving in the military, specifically in the Minnesota National Guard. Before he did so, he asked me if I was comfortable with that. I said yes.

In between Governor Walz's speaking with civilians and soldiers, Jensen introduced me to him. This is the impact of supportive leadership, from the highest level to the most direct. From the time I came out to my immediate supervisor, a first lieutenant, to becoming a full-time soldier with the support of a two-star general, I've felt like a valuable member of this organization.

The Minnesota National Guard is dedicated to its soldiers and airmen and has actively demonstrated this commitment in many ways, including being the first state to work with an LGBTQ magazine for advertising and stories. It is the only state that I'm aware of that has added a rainbow to its social media profiles for Pride month in 2018. The MNNG has been visible and vocal about supporting LGBTQ people at a time when our president [was] not. Behind the scenes, the Diversity and Inclusion Office also has an LGBTQ Special Emphasis Council that works with other civilian organizations and businesses in the state.

Because of my admiration for the people with whom I serve I have chosen to sign another six-year contract with the Minnesota National Guard. I've been asked by people in the LGBTQ community, How am I able to serve under our current administration? I've thought about this a lot, especially when I had the opportunity to leave at the end of my first six-year contract. It goes back to the people. The support in Minnesota is great, and I feel that I can make a bigger difference leading and serving by example rather than from the outside.

Zaneford Alvarez, Sergeant, U.S. Army, 2012–present

I've been an Army brat my whole life. My dad is still on active duty as a recruiter. I'm Sergeant Alvarez, he's Sergeant Major Alvarez. One of the reasons that I'm proud to be in the Army is because it's a family business. It's not just my dad and I either. All of my grandfather's kids have served in the military at one point in time, be it the reserves, in the Guard, or active duty. He himself served and retired as a full-bird colonel. I've got a great picture of all three of us in dress uniforms. I hate to brag, but it is one of my favorite pictures. It's the only picture I have of all three of us together in our uniforms and I'm wearing my male dress uniform. Great picture. It's very surreal to think about the uniform I now wear. It's the same uniform that my dad wears, same pair of boots, same hat. Down to our name. It's all the same. I'm very proud to serve.

I joined the military straight out of high school. My dad was very candid with me about Army life, but I still said yes because I saw it as a stepping-stone to moving forward with my life. I graduated high school in June 2012, and left for basic training a month later. I was at Fort Gordon from the time I was eighteen until just before I turned twenty-two, and it was very much a time for learning.

I chose the military occupational specialty that I hold now, behavioral health technician. I didn't really know much about that career field, but I went with it. I ended up falling in love with it when I went through the school. After completing training, I went to Fort Gordon, where I worked at the hospital unit. I worked in outpatient behavioral health and inpatient psychiatry. I've done a wide variety of things, including patient escorts, psych testing, and working with substance abuse patients. I was really fortunate with the opportunities that came my way as they helped me figure out who I was and who I wanted to be, particularly with regard to my gender identity. When, in 2015, my hospital held a Christmas party, I decided I wanted to begin my transition from female to male, so, as we were required to wear civilian clothes, I wore jeans with a button-up shirt, vest, and a tie. I felt good. I looked good. But I was obviously anxious and, in front of behavioral health providers, it showed. I thought, "Someone's going to say something. I can't really hide it." Then a captain pulled me aside. It was not out of malicious intent; she was very nice. She was asking me what was going on, and I tried to dismiss the conversation, but she dragged it out of me. I told her, "I'm about to start medically transitioning." Although the ban hadn't actually been lifted yet, nobody was being discharged for being trans. I received a lot of positive feedback from her. She first apologized, saying, "I'm so sorry for calling you by the wrong pronouns this whole time." This captain was saying this to little junior enlisted me, apologizing to *me*. I can't even begin to tell you what that felt like. She was really supportive of the situation and all. We went back to the party, and everything was normal.

I didn't know at the time, but afterwards she ended up talking with all of the other residents and interns about referring to me by male pronouns. None of them had a problem with it and soon all the first lieutenants and captains were calling me by male pronouns. I wasn't used to it. It just brought a smile on my face. But then my non-commissioned officer in charge (NCOIC) found out, and he was livid. I think he just didn't grasp the whole situation and saw what people were doing and thought that I was *making* them call me by male pronouns. One specific thing that he said at the time was, "At the end of the day, you go by what your paperwork says. It says female. And there's not a goddamn thing you can do to change that." That hurt.

Because of the negative and toxic leadership I experienced at Fort Gordon, I told myself that I was either going to get stationed in Germany or I was going to get out. I did end up in Germany, where I was assigned a sponsor to assist with my relocation. My sponsor was also a specialist who was living in the barracks and, since according to my paperwork I was still "female," my sponsor was female. Although I was nervous about the move and my transition, I wasn't sure what I should or could say. I ended up sharing with her that I was transitioning and that by the time I would arrive in Germany, I would have been on testosterone for five months. I told her that I would be reaching a point where I wouldn't be able to hide it and expected that by then I would look and sound male. I already cut my hair short. After the conversation, she told the section NCOIC. Her name was Sergeant Major Haines and I will never forget her. After my experience at Fort Gordon, I honestly wasn't expecting anything whatsoever from leadership. If they were not going to support me, I just wanted to know that before I even arrived.

Not long after that, while still at Fort Gordon, I was told there was a sergeant major on the phone for me. It was my future boss, Sergeant Major Haines. She said, "Okay, I want to know from you, your situation." She's a very tough and powerful woman. She's scary as shit, but I love her, but at the time I didn't know what to expect. She was asking me all of these questions, trying to understand my situation, and get a sense of what she should expect to see when I arrive. I told her everything. I was honest with her about what was coming, and she offered nothing but support and positivity. It was, "We got you. Now I know. Now I understand. I've got your back. You have my full support. And if anybody gives you issues, you let me know." That was the end of it. From company level all the way to the brigade commander, it was nothing but positivity from my leadership. There were a couple of people in the beginning of the unit who referred to me by female pronouns but, after a while, either the situation was addressed in my favor or they had moved away.

Before, during, and after the policy change, I experienced, and continue to experience, a lot of support. My gender marker hasn't changed yet. I'm still waiting until the Army tells me that they recognize me as male. However, my experience in Germany was about feeling respect for the first time. Really feeling it. Respect is part of the Army values, and while I've definitely given respect based on rank and position, that was my first time really receiving it. It was my first time that a unit made me feel like a valued member of the team and that included people that I hadn't even met in person, only via phone and email. I experienced more compassion and understanding from them than I did in the three years that I spent with my unit in Georgia. I've been doing great since making the move. And now, three and a half years into transition, including one year post–top surgery, I'm feeling great.

For me and other transgender service members, it's always been about wanting to serve honorably and being recognized and respected for who we are. Being transgender doesn't negatively impact or impede our service. Despite having all of those issues with my leadership in my last unit, there was never a negative impact on me doing my job as a behavioral health technician. I've never once felt that it negatively impacted my work. I always let my coworkers know that despite being trans, "I'm here to do a job just like you. I'm here to be a part of this team, just like you. Nothing is going to stop me from continuing to move forward and serving with honor, and I've done that for the last seven years of being in."

Probably the biggest impact of transitioning is that I no longer care about trying to please people, I just do the things I need to do to excel. Instead of worrying so much about all these little things, being myself allowed me to do things I wanted to do. One of the things I wanted to do was to try to earn an EFMB, the Expert Field Medical Badge. While participating in this competition I needed to live in another set of barracks, so I let people that that I needed to be listed as female and assigned to the female barracks. Remember, I may have "looked" like the guy that I was, but I was "officially" still female. Well, I was basically laughed at. Throughout the whole time of in-processing, my situation wasn't taken seriously whatsoever.

I finally completed in-processing and I'm slowly mustering up whatever courage I have to get ready to walk into the bay (sleeping/living area), the giant female bay of all the other people who were going out for this badge. These are people all over Europe, including some from NATO allies as well. And I just said to myself, "Fuck it, I'm just going to knock them all out at once." Before walking in, I was trying to think, how quickly is someone going to stop me from walking into the female bay? I think it happened within about three seconds of my walking into the bay. "Excuse me, this is the female bay, you can't be in here." And

I'm like, "Okay, got it." I walked to the center of the room and said, "Can I have everybody's attention please, everybody come closer." I'm probably one of the lowest-ranking people there. I had sergeants, sergeants first class, other specialists and privates, lieutenants, captains, majors, all of these people staring at me. I was quick and brief and informative. "Okay, I'm just getting you all at once, explaining this once, so you know." I outed myself because I just wanted to get it over with so people weren't confused. "I am a transgender soldier, born female, transitioning to male. I enlisted as female. I have to be here. These are the buildings I'm assigned to. If there are any questions or concerns, please address them to me directly." And of all the reactions that I got, someone in the back says, "Hell yeah." What? *That* caught me off guard!

I experienced no issues with any of the other soldiers with whom I competed. Some people actually took the time to come and talk with me and ask me questions, which is exactly what I had hoped. I put that out there. I'd rather you ask than assume. Some people even asked for advice. How would I address this with a soldier? What is the best course of action, or how can I offer a soldier in this situation the best support possible? In the end, it was a more positive experience because of the people with whom I was competing. I'm still friends with one of them that actually got the badge. Sadly, I did not get the badge, but I will try again if the opportunity comes.

When I returned to my unit, Sergeant Major Haines asked me how everything went. Of course, I told her everything that happened, the good and the bad. I told her about how someone in the cadre felt compelled to purchase shower curtains because they didn't like me being in the showers with the women. The sergeant major was pissed, which is never a good thing. She was very upset at the poor level of leadership displayed by those NCOs and, reportedly, some people got in trouble. She was basically apologizing for them. And she was asking me if I wanted them to apologize to me, and I said no. I don't want an apology. I don't give apologies. I never liked apologies because, more often than not, they're not genuine. I told her to handle it how you would want it handled. She had my back and that made me very happy. In fact, I presented her with what's called a SPARTA coin. SPARTA is a trans service member group and the coin they created is used in a variety of settings to recognize excellence. One side of the SPARTA coin said, "It's not what we do, but how we do it that distinguishes us." The other side said, "Veni, Vidi, Vici" and "30 June 2016," the date that Secretary Carter had announced a policy of inclusion. I give these coins to people like Sergeant Major Haines who are true allies. The people that I consider true allies are those leaders that I have come in contact with in the past, who contact me again when they have a transgender soldier and want to know how they can help. Those are the people we need the most. Those people, like Sergeant Major Haines, deserve that kind of recognition.

Another person I presented a coin to was Colonel Neumeier. She was the best, most badass, awesome, short little nurse from Texas. When someone made comments or jokes she considered to be very inappropriate, she became very pissed. If you were assaulted or harassed, Colonel Neumeier, like Sergeant Major Haines, was the person to talk with. Like Sergeant Major Haines, Colonel Neumeier asked if I wanted an apology and again I said, "No." However, the trainer did email an apology, copying all of the people that had attended that training. She said, essentially, "It was never my intent to disrespect Sergeant Alvarez and his situation about being transgender." Although nothing she said made it better, this is another example of good leadership.

I've told my story a lot and I'm going to keep telling it because this is another perspective. I'm not just another transgender person. I am Zane, I'm something else. And I'm not any less human.

Caroline A. Morrison, Specialist, U.S. Army National Guard, 1999–Present

For so much of my life, I was obsessed about being the first anything. My dream was to make a difference or impact history in some way. As I sat in history class I would listen to the stories of the visionaries who did something special, seeing it define their legacy. Rosa Parks protested, Neil Armstrong walked on the moon, John F. Kennedy was elected the first Catholic president, and Edison and Tesla invented. Others made history in groups, and because those groups were made based on who they were, their names are rarely remembered, but all of them did something that separated them from others for the rest of time.

I wanted that so much for myself. I desperately wanted to be a first. I joined my high school's swim team in its second year and was the first "male" to swim the breaststroke. Though I'm certain they were broken long ago, every time I swam I broke my previous record in that stroke. On a deployment to Djibouti, I liked to point out that I was the only Army chaplain's assistant on the continent at that time. I strove in my life not simply to be the best, but to try to find a way to be the first to do something, always imagining that I would wind up in a book somewhere. But, for all my research, all of my years of trying to find ways to make an impact and leave a legacy, my biggest contribution may actually come from finally coming out and living authentically.

Like so many of my trans "siblings," I have known most of my life that I wasn't the boy I was being raised to be, though I did my best to live like I was. After all, in 1999, when I enlisted, being homo- or trans- anything was enough to get you put out of the military. My plan to have a career in the Army and to be a pastor in the civilian world depended on my presenting as a cisgender, heterosexual man. But my NCOIC once found my stash of women's clothing and informed my first sergeant, thus ending my time on active duty. In April 2001, I found myself a civilian once again.

In 2004, after a few years of college and having married, I joined the National Guard. I had decided then that I would do everything in my power to repress the woman hidden inside me. In many ways I was the object of my own oppression. I lived for years hiding who I was and letting her out only on certain occasions. I shaved my legs on deployments just so I could see a piece of her. Then, in December 2015, my wife found my clothing stash and asked me if I was transgender. Finally, I said yes.

In 2015, transgender people were still forbidden from serving in the military. I had heard that there were some trans people serving, albeit while hiding, and that within my state a colonel had transitioned in the final years of her service. I, however, wasn't quite ready to test that. The announcement that the policy would be changing raised the possibility of being open. But, due to my civilian job, I wasn't in a place to take advantage of that. November 2016 changed everything. The election of our forty-fifth president led me to a place where I was forced into prayer out of a directionless confusion and led me to confront my truth and the idea that I was called to serve authentically—rather than the half existence I was living at that time. I told my wife of the understanding that I had come to and we decided, along with my therapist, that I would begin my medical transition in February 2017.

Because of an agreement I made with my civilian employer, during the first few months I transitioned in hiding. Then, in May 2017, I came out to the Army. In doing so, I achieved my dream; I became the first soldier in the Kansas National Guard to transition under the new, inclusive policy; the first trans person in my military occupational specialty in the state; and the first openly transgender member of my unit. I remember being so nervous when I sat down with my commander, but he was incredibly professional. If he was surprised, he didn't reveal it. He took the information I had and then we went about our business. Over the next few months, I came out to several other people in the unit. Even among those I knew held very different political ideologies, I found professionals who continued to treat me like the soldier I was.

The history books always tell the stories of the "firsts." They show pictures of black children being escorted into their newly integrated school. They tell the story of the riots at Stonewall. They tell the tale of the impact that firsts have on history, but they don't tell the impact that being first had on the person. Being first meant that I came out to my command in May 2017 after having been medically transitioning for three months, knowing the procedure but having no precedent to know what reaction to expect. Coming out was life-changing/life-giving. A weight was lifted from my shoulders, as I told my commander. The meeting was wonderful. However, it was the precursor to a year of frustration as the policy stopped simply being something on a piece of paper and started entering the implementation phase.

I didn't encounter blatant transphobia, but I had numerous leaders tell me that while they didn't agree or understand, they would act as professionals. When, in late July of 2017, the president sent his tweets proposing a ban on all transgender military service, I was heartbroken. I loved the military and was so close to retirement, but I didn't know if I could go back in the closet at that point. Even with that internal turmoil, nothing changed at my unit. When the tweets came, none of my leadership, not even the chaplain, reached out to see how I was doing or to make sure I was doing alright. I didn't receive support or expressions of opposition. There was just silence.

I existed in a strange dichotomy where I was living as myself, a lesbian woman, twenty-eight days a month, but I had to get a haircut, stop wearing makeup, ensure the changes happening were as concealed as possible, and put my male persona back on for the two to three days of drill. Eventually, the monthly ebb and flow of male and female took its toll and I reached out to my commander. Something as seemingly innocuous as a haircut was hugely problematic for me. I may have cut it for drill, but that male haircut then stayed around all month until the next haircut the following month. This was having an impact on my ability to see me and was a dysphoria-inducing reminder that there was a major part of my life, my unit, that only saw me as a "male" soldier. I asked my commander to help me find a haircut that he could live with and that I could "re"-style to live authentically—as the woman I was—the rest of the time. He obliged by simply saying, "Just keep it in the regulation." He was referring to the male hair standards found in Army Regulation 670–1, and he was giving me permission to sit on the edges of the regulation so long as I didn't go over them. So I got a pixie that I could adjust for both personas.

During that time, I found solace and sisterhood with most of the other women in my unit. They accepted me and saw me as me. After a long day pretending to be someone else, it was being able to be me around them that really saved me. I recall one incident as particularly draining. In the military we have periodic physicals to ensure we are in good health. Laying on a table for my electrocardiogram with my T-shirt off and wearing only my shorts and sports bra wasn't enough to be gendered properly—that is, as a woman. They did what they were supposed to, they followed the regulation. It really drove home the impact "being polite" could have on a person's mental health. Calling me "sir" was socially polite, but hugely dysphoric that day. I went to my friends afterwards and spent time being me. It did everything to raise my morale. However, at the end of the day, I had to leave my support system because I wasn't allowed to stay with them due to my gender marker still being an M.

I did everything I could to survive during that time. When I was prevented from going on my unit's deployment because of my history of kidney stones, I once again worked to keep my morale up. From May 2017 to February 2018, I kept trying to serve while the equal opportunity office tried to help everyone understand exactly what their roles were, what was and what wasn't allowed, and what the future truly looked like. Time really felt as though it was dragging, because everyone involved was learning. Nothing was happening fast enough.

In the Army, there are three unofficial names for the phases of training: crawl, walk, and run. Where I needed people to be in walk or run, everyone was still crawling. The frustration of both sides seemed to come to a head in February 2018 when I asked for lodging accommodations. I had been medically transitioning for a year and because of the effects of my second puberty, I no longer felt that being in an open bay with the male soldiers was a comfortable or safe environment. The response, ultimately, was to transfer me to a new unit.

I had lived in Kansas for nearly twenty years at that point, but arriving in my new unit was the first time I truly understood the overwhelming relief that Dorothy Gale must have felt to suddenly find herself in the technicolor of Oz. Oz wasn't just accepting, it was affirming. I was told to show up to my first drill as me, that my days of changing who I was for drill were over. It's interesting looking back at how my attitude toward the military changed just by experiencing affirmation and acceptance from my unit and command. That helped me so much, because I was no longer fighting to be myself. I was seen and treated as me. As soon as my paperwork came in for my name and gender change, it was taken care of, and no one really thought much of it, because I was already me for all of them.

So I sit here now having completed my transition in the Army. I'm not me because of an exception to policy anymore. I'm not me because my colleagues are nice enough to use my pronouns. I am simply me. I suppose that is the other difficult thing about being a first for simply being yourself. The students during integration are remembered for being the first black children to attend "white" schools, not for any personal accomplishments. I was known more for being transgender. My accomplishments didn't seem to matter. It warps your identity when you are only known for who you are and not for what you have done.

As time has passed, I have been able to once again be seen for my professional contributions. And that's the other thing about being a first—as you move into history, you can look back and watch as life is improved for those after you. Since I came out, there have been numerous soldiers who have come out. And while they might experience some of the attitudes I did, I know they won't experience most of the same hiccups and frustrations I have. In being myself, I have left a legacy. In being myself, I have made history. In being myself, I was able to have an impact on those who came after me. Few things are quite as amazing to me as the knowledge that, after all my searching, it was in being myself that I found my historical first.

Mak Vaden, Warrant Officer 1, U.S. Army National Guard, 2006–present

I am a thirty-year-old transgender soldier with twelve years of honorable service. I currently serve on active duty orders with the National Guard. In 2006, after my first year of college, I enlisted in the reserves. Shortly thereafter I left school and entered active duty, serving until 2010 when I returned to the Georgia Army National Guard. I've been in the Guard ever since. Prior to coming out as transgender I served the first several years of my career under "Don't Ask, Don't Tell," hiding my sexual orientation out of the constant fear of expulsion. I then found myself in the same predicament as when I first joined, wanting nothing more than to serve my country and do my job, but at the cost of sacrificing a major part of who I am. This, on top of all the other things *every* service member sacrifices such as time with loved ones, wear and tear on the body and mind, etc. This time, however, I decided that I could no longer sacrifice my own well-being, my own authentic self. This time there was no going back, even though at the time I made that decision there was no protection from expulsion, an expulsion that would have cost me my career, professional goals, and any future contribution I could make to my country as a service member. Past feelings of anxiety, fear, depression, resentment, anger, and many more came back like a flashback from war. In fact, I felt as though that would have been preferable as eventually you return from the flashbacks into reality. My reality was an ongoing flashback from which there appeared to be no escape. I had no problem waking up on deployments knowing that could be the day I die, because I knew I would have done something with my life and would die doing what I love. But to wake up not knowing if that would be the day the organization to which you have given your adult life will abandon you is unbearable. Having wrestled with these issues, I made the decision to submit my paperwork to the military to have my name and gender marker changed.

Since that time, I have paid for every penny of my medical treatment out of pocket, partly out of fear that the president's continuous attacks on transgender service members would eventually succeed, and partly out of personal principle and pride. I was informed by human resources personnel that doing a gender change could require an eighteen-month "stabilization" period. I submitted a request for a waiver so that I can deploy with my unit and do the job I love. I do it for the brothers and sisters in arms I also love. I do the job for which the American taxpayers have paid. Over the course of my career, I have consistently increased my physical fitness test scores, fired sharpshooter at the range, and have received several awards. More specifically, I have accomplished this during my transition period, which many apparently think is the time transgender service members are the most "unstable" and "vulnerable." My specific accomplishments serve as evidence to the contrary.

I am in no way trying to say I am a perfect soldier. I have certainly made my fair share of mistakes over the years. I've been late to formation and have, on occasion, during a long and tedious training convoy neglected to wear my Kevlar (personal body armor). What I am saying, however, is that I am more than capable of performing my job as a soldier and a non-commissioned officer. In 2015, I was nominated by my first sergeant to compete for NCO of the Year. I think the many accomplishments, courses, scores, and other results have demonstrated that I have not just survived the damning DADT, and now the president's transgender ban, but I have thrived in spite of them. I served on active duty in Iraq. I served at the Texas/Mexico border on a Texas Army National Guard border mission. I served in the Hurricane Irma response force, and I have volunteered for countless off duty training, mission, and public relations taskings. I have both learned and grown a lot from them all. I plan on continuing to do so. Even now I am sitting in my barracks room in the middle of a training course grieving my grandfather who passed a couple of days ago. But I'm also trying to push through the pain and the fear of the "what ifs" of having submitted my paperwork for my gender marker change so that I may accomplish the mission.

I have invested countless days/weeks/months/years of blood, sweat, tears, and heart into my job, my unit, my soldiers, and my country. I have endured countless hours of fear, anxiety, depression, and anger and countless ignorant/hateful/discriminatory comments. Some were face to face, though most were when people thought I wasn't listening. Although I am not a religious person I am very spiritual and believe in a higher power. I have come to peace with the fact that what is going to happen is going to happen and whatever is meant to be, will be. It is my hope and dream that both those in the military who review my files and the unseen/unspoken one on a spiritual level determine that I am able to charlie mike—continue mission, for you nonmilitary folk. That is, that I am able to continue serving my country. I intend to accomplish whatever mission the future has in store, be it continuing to serve in the military or being expelled and serving in a police or fire-fighting force in my community.

It has now been a year and a half since I submitted my gender marker change packet, and I am still waiting for it to finish making its way through the system. It is tedious, frustrating, and keeps the fear of bias, bigotry, and unjust obstacles being placed in the way of my career from prejudiced leadership alive in my head and heart. Despite this, though, I know I will get to keep my career. I am one of the lucky ones who jumped through all the systematic hoops and maneuvered my way through the red tape to ensure I was grandfathered in under the Carter policy. Although I will not feel truly secure until my gender marker packet is fully processed, I am grateful that I do not have to fear for my career every day and weep for those who are being denied the opportunity to be themselves and serve their country. Our military readiness remains compromised so long as those willing and able to serve are not allowed to do so due to politicized prejudice. The core principles of our country of liberty, equality, and justice for all also remain compromised while this ban is in place.

The strength of our military and our country comes not only from our diversity, but from what we must do to overcome those who oppose that diversity, those who continue to engage in discrimination against those who differ from themselves. History, both the nation's and my own, is a testament to that and the current transgender ban is no exception. Regardless of what's in store for me, I know I have joined another army, one that is fighting and will continue to fight for the rights of all. As veterans and current service members know, they can take you out of the battle, the war, or the military all they want, but they *cannot* take the fight out of you. I hope that my story doesn't just resound with others but lights a fire in them, offering camaraderie and comfort in knowing they aren't alone in their risks, struggles, and fears. I hope it lights their way forward amidst the darkness of this ban. I hope that it keeps the fire burning, eliminating the obstacles that get in their way, ultimately allowing them to thrive despite the adversity they face.

Tucker Duval, Captain, U.S. Army, 2008–2017

When I came across the opportunity to submit an essay to this volume, I pounced. For better or worse, completing the forty-seven-month West Point experience and serving five years as an engineer officer in the U.S. Army has dominated my adult life. Serving as a trans man both before and after the ban was lifted added an extra dimension to an already hopelessly complex experience for me. I have expended so much mental and emotional energy trying to make sense of my Army experience, both while I was going through it and ever since I left; sometimes it seems like it's all I can think about. I figured the things I'd have to say for this essay would be spilling from my fingertips faster than I could type. Instead, I spent months staring at that cheeky little blinking cursor presiding over the vast nothing I could get on the page.

Writer's block is always frustrating, but I was particularly flummoxed and annoyed by my inability to find my voice on this extremely salient topic. How many times had I been walking to my car, having been turned away by yet another health care professional at Fort Hood, wailing inside (also sometimes aloud) about how much I needed to tell my story? I wanted so badly for a platform on which to tell the outside world about what the crazy-making, hall of mirrors Army medical system was doing to me and how devastating it was. As I suffered in isolation, I dreamt about exposing to the world the cruelty and inanity of a system that barely even registered my existence. And yet, presented at last with the opportunity to share my story, I struggled to find even the first word.

The truth is, I'm not sure I really see the point in telling that story anymore. To be sure, I believe it is a valuable story. Stories are the building blocks of our lives and identities, and this was a big one for me. But the story of my trans Army experience echoes and overlaps that of almost every other trans person with whom I served. My experiences were singularly frustrating and painful *to me* because I was the one enduring them, but they were far from unique. The same kind of things happened to the majority of similarly situated folks, and many people endured much more trying hardships than I did. I had many factors working to my advantage—my whiteness, my status as an officer, my reputation as an accomplished soldier, the fact that I came out in my last year of service and thus always had the comfort of knowing that, no matter how bleak things seemed, my exit to the brighter beyond was imminent. I had the vigorous support of my brigade commander and my doctor, both of whom did their utmost to help me. Even so, I spent a full year trying and failing over and over again to start the hormone replacement therapy to which I was entitled, and I never even made it to the right specialist's office. I lost count of the number of appointments with doctors and psychiatrists and psychologists and social workers that resulted in the same tired, demoralizing end: I can't help you. It was like dealing with the customer service department of a business that you know is perversely incentivized to give you bad customer service, only instead of an hour-long infuriating phone call, it was a yearlong waking nightmare.

But this is the frame of a story that undergirds hundreds, if not thousands, of trans service members who were trying to seek the medically necessary care to which we were entitled throughout 2016 and 2017. Ultimately, it's a story of flaccid half measures and painfully mismanaged incrementalism. It's a story about institutional feet dragging and its real-life effects. And, although it's certainly a story of how the Army inexcusably failed me, I've come to realize since I left active duty that, as terrible as that was, it wasn't the worst thing the Army did to me. I'm still coming to terms with all the ways that being in the Army hurt me. In that ongoing processing, I'm still figuring out how I think about and relate to service in the American armed forces, both personally and politically. I'm still trying to understand how I can support the trans people serving in the military while staunchly opposing the institutions in which they serve. Whenever I try to find a coherent position, I'm reminded of the phrase tossed about in my childhood church whenever the topic of homosexuality came up: "We have to hate the sin but love the sinner." It makes me feel like I'm wearing a mantle cut from the same hypocrisy cloth as that sentiment. How can I construct a story that honors the nobility and self-sacrifice underpinning individuals' willingness to serve others, while condemning the predatory, violent, and fundamentally anti-queer vehicles in which they choose to do it?

Many social constructs, like gender, are so old, so widespread that they can appear as if they are found truths about the world rather than things that people made up at some point. They are so deeply embedded in our collective conscience that most people feel them more like skin than like clothing. This is especially true for those of us who are predisposed, whether by personality or conditioning, to viewing the world we find around us as normative—that is, a propensity to believe that how things currently are is how they ought to be. From this vantage point, almost anything that is viewed as "wrong" would best be righted by a return to "the way things used to be"—a nostalgia-tinged idea of yesteryear.

This way of viewing and interacting with social norms is the predominant mode in military culture, at both the institutional and individual levels. Respect, even reverence, for dominant American cultural norms *and* for the practice of adhering to said norms is in the very DNA of military life. The institution of the military rests upon a foundation of strict, unquestioning adherence to internal norms, commonly referred to as "meeting the standard." "The standard" is military speak for a norm or a regulation, depending on the context. And there is a standard for everything: how you cut your hair, how you wear your clothes, how you clean and arrange your barracks room, how you maintain your personally owned vehicle, and how you inhabit your own body.

A belief in the realness and rightness of the gender binary is a foundational predicate of the Army appearance and grooming standards as well as behavioral expectations. Army Regulation 670–1, which governs uniforms, appearance, and grooming standards, contains provisions that are punitive. That is, under the Uniform Code of Military Justice, adverse actions can be brought against soldiers who violate these standards. The regulations concerning haircuts, jewelry, cosmetics, and fingernail length are all coded with traditional, "acceptable" expressions of either of two acknowledged binary genders.

These regulations exist ostensibly to maintain uniformity throughout the ranks. A reasonable person might wonder how, for example, a man choosing to wear studs in his ears would disrupt uniformity more so than a woman doing the same, but even if we concede that this need for uniformity is one purpose of these regulations, it seems clear to me that the most important, if the least articulated, function here is to uphold a particular kind of masculinity that has prevailed in military institutions for centuries. These rules prescribe a certain kind of femininity and a certain kind of masculinity and they brook no ambiguity, no divergence, no nuance. They expressly prohibit male soldiers from exhibiting female coded forms of expression. They tell men how it is acceptable to express their masculinity and women their femininity, backed by the weight and force of military law.

The gender binary is ultimately a tool that patriarchies and patriarchal power structures use to maintain male hegemony. The military, in turn, serves to solidify that hegemony by uniformly adopting and internally enforcing our beloved patriarchy's gender mythology—as well as, of course, by propagating American power and "values" abroad. The military may be able to grudgingly tolerate the presence of transgender service members, but, by its very constitution, I find myself believing that it will never be able to celebrate them or offer them the right to unqualified, unbridled self-determination that is the birthright of every human being on earth. I am starting to feel like it impossible to be both pro-queer and pro-military.

There are gaps in this account where advocates for transgender military service would hasten to step in and counter my perspective. I imagine opponents crying, "Military service requires sacrifice, and everyone, even cis/straight service members sacrifice their right to individuality and self-expression." Perhaps this is true, if one accepts that the American military and the ways in which it is deployed is actually in either the national interest or in the people's interest. "There are so many trans people who want desperately to serve, and they deserve the right to do so the same as anyone else," some might say. This is also true. I have served with and come to know many trans service members, some who remained closeted and some who served openly, who led long, successful, and fulfilling careers. Far be it from me to deny anyone the opportunity to do the work they are called to do, and shame on anyone who tells a trans person that they are unqualified to do any kind of work simply because they are trans.

And yet I still struggle to bring my full effort to this particular fight. After a stretch of difficult reflection, I think I'm beginning to understand why. Denying me the right to serve openly as a trans man, with access to the medical care I needed to transition, was not the worst way the Army was bad for me. When I left for West Point at eighteen, I was a turtle that had spent a lifetime in its shell. I had no idea who I was or what was possible for me because I'd never had the freedom to explore the world outside the dark, cramped safety of my shell. By the time I started to figure me out, I was already trapped in an institution that cared absolutely nothing for my development as a person or my ability to live a good life.

To me, the Army was a prison. It was a prison to which I had willingly submitted, but I had done so on the basis of abominably incomplete and inaccurate information about what I was getting into. And there was no way out—no early release for good behavior, no possibility of parole. It stole time and opportunities away from me. It turned my early adulthood into one long trial to be endured. It stunted my growth and warped my sense of self and of the world. It trampled on my humanity in a myriad of ways, large and small. But no matter how grand or how trivial the indignities, I felt them all—every time I was denied a say or a choice or a vote, some essential part of me suffocated. I learned to live with it after a while, and through it all I was a decent, dutiful officer, but I cannot think of the Army with any fondness, nor wish that life upon anyone I care about.

The trans equality movement is large and diverse and I believe there is room for everyone to contribute in unique, authentic ways. These days, I'd rather be saving trans people from the military than trying to get them in. I think we'd all be a little better off with a lot less of the American military in our lives and in our hearts.

Nate Hoang, Captain, U.S. Army, 2017–present

JOURNAL ENTRY, JULY 1, 2016

Yesterday I got a notification on my phone from the SPARTA group on Facebook. All of us in the group were waiting expectantly for news to drop about the transgender military ban.

When I found out that Secretary of Defense Ash Carter ended the ban on transgender Americans in the military, I felt relieved. The relief came in waves. By the end of the day, I felt drained. It felt similar to when I finished taking the last exam in finals week. I was relieved, happy, and tired. I felt abnormally tired by the time I went home. The news was sinking in, and as it sunk in, my relief manifested as exhaustion.

Kim and I celebrated by going out to eat. It was a happy exhaustion, as if I had been carrying the burden of a hazy future that was once so certain.

I was burdened by the what-ifs of being transgender in the military. In spring 2011, I decided to apply for the Health Professions Scholarship

Program after doing thorough research on military dentistry during the previous winter break. In summer 2011, I took my Dental Admissions Test. I also decided that, if I was to be a good soldier, I needed to focus on fitness, so I began working out in earnest early in 2011. I did my first pull-up that spring. I was determined from that point forward to do everything I needed to receive the scholarship and eventually to be a military dentist.

I had reservations about being in the military in 2011—mostly about my physical capabilities, but, underneath everything, whether I would be socially accepted within the perceived strict military confines of hierarchy and regulations. In 2011, I hadn't fully embraced or understood my queerness. Nevertheless, I was so happy that the "Don't Ask, Don't Tell" policy was repealed that year. Moving forward, I knew that I would not have to be afraid about being out as a gay person in the military. That comforted me.

In April 2013, after being admitted to dental school, I joined the Army as an officer. It was one of the happiest moments of my life for a few reasons. One reason was that I accomplished the goal I set years prior to that moment. Another was the wonderful relief of starting the journey to becoming a military dentist. Repeating the oath after my recruiter was a beautiful moment that I will always remember.

I took pride in the fact that I will eventually serve in the military. I worked hard in dental school so that I could be a good military dentist.

My foundation was shaken when, in 2014, I began thinking deeply about my gender identity and about my queerness in relation to what it means to be transgender. When it finally clicked that I am transgender, my little world of certainty crumbled. I learned that being transgender in the military was not allowed. Though I was lucky to live in a time where I could connect with others like me through the Internet, all transgender service members were at risk of being discharged simply because of their gender identity.

I began to question why I was in the military in the first place. No longer could I be as proud as I had been about being in the military. I couldn't be in the face of a transgender ban. I knew that I might lose my scholarship and my career in the military. There was no timeline for a repeal of the ban. I had no idea if I would have to repay my education to the Army by taking out loans or whether I would have to serve in silence about my identity.

The main roadblock to being open about myself was the ban. My employer maintained that I am not allowed to be a soldier, thus I hesitated on transitioning. I cried. I confided in my dear friends. Eventually I decided that, even if it meant losing my career, I had to choose survival.

Yesterday the ban was lifted. I can now be open—I can completely embrace who I am to everyone in the military and let them know that I am transgender and proud of it. I can serve without risk of losing my job. The education that the Army has invested in me can be put into good use as I serve others as a dentist for the foreseeable future. I can again dream about having a career in the military. We have so much more work to do, but for right now, I am going to celebrate this wonderful moment.

* * *

In summer 2017, I went on active duty and attended the Basic Officer Leaders Course (BOLC) in San Antonio, Texas. I went to San Antonio, my mind set on staying hydrated so that I don't become a heat casualty, like I did that one time in the fifth grade when I passed out after running a mile in my oversized Gap hoodie. I had begun to wear the hoodie as a way to hide my growing chest, despite the chance of overheating during PT (physical training).

The incoming class of assorted health care professionals and students were grouped into platoons. On the first day, we were told to introduce ourselves with one fact that not many people know about ourselves. In the spur of the moment, I decided to come out, consequences be damned. I said, as confidently as I could, "My name is Nate Hoang. One thing that not many people know about me is that I am transgender. I am an intersectional feminist, so if you ever have any questions, feel free to ask me." I am glad that I came out in such a public way. I felt seen, and I made genuine connections while I was at BOLC.

Time came for me to move to my first duty station, to Ft. Carson. On the morning of my first day of in-processing, I found out about the current transgender service member ban put forth via Twitter. The news crushed me. It felt as if my career was grounded before it had a chance to take off.

Many emotions came up, including betrayal. I worked so hard to get here—to be able to serve as a dentist. I had the same education as my co-residents, yet I was the only one who could effectively be fired, solely for being transgender.

Increasingly, I felt pushed back into the closet. Where a couple of months prior, I was proudly able to share my identity with others, now I was compelled to keep quiet about it out of fear that it would further jeopardize my career.

In this state of uncertainty, I felt that I needed to let my leadership know where I stood, so I sent my commander the following letter:

AUG 9, 2017

Dear COL _____,

It was a pleasure meeting you the other day. I am so fortunate to be [in the program]. I am excited to learn and practice dentistry this upcoming year and to look back this time next year, hopefully amazed at the progress I have made.

I am humbled by what you advised me at our meeting: to avoid making critical mistakes in practice, and to be empathetic toward my patients. I take your advice to heart and I will do my best to achieve both goals over this year and for the rest of my career.

There is something that has been weighing heavily on my heart since Wednesday, July 26, that I wanted to share with you. It's important for me to be open and honest with you so that I can better serve under your command.

On Wednesday, July 26, President Trump tweeted that he would ban transgender service. As a transgender man, I was stunned that I would no longer be allowed to serve should the tweet become policy.

During my second year of dental school, I finally allowed myself to exist in my truest gender after years of struggling with my gender identity. At that time, the transgender ban was still in place, and I had to make the difficult decision to prioritize my health over potentially losing my scholarship and my career in the military. My future would have been dark had I not pursued receiving care to alleviate my gender dysphoria.

Fortunately, the ban was lifted before I would enter Active Duty, and with all my official documents updated to reflect my name and gender, I was also able to change my gender marker in DEERS right before BOLC (Basic Officer Leaders Course) with the help of our command surgeon.

I was advised by the command surgeon to receive a diagnosis for gender dysphoria for official Army records as soon as I get to my first duty station. I have begun the process to obtain a diagnosis and to continue receiving medical care here at Ft. Carson.

I have gone through many emotions—fear, sadness, frustration— since that Wednesday, but I am operating on the hope that the ban will never come to fruition and that I can continue to do my job—and do it well. I would be more than grateful to have the full support of my command as I move forward. I want to be the very best Army dentist I can be, and I believe that I can achieve my goals with your support and mentorship.

I am always available to speak with you in person, through phone, or via email if there is anything you would like to communicate, or if you have any questions for me.

Sincerely,

Nate Hoang

* * *

As the freedom to be myself was rescinded, I also retreated from social media and isolated myself. If I had triumphantly put the closet door behind me just a year ago, I had to go back into the closet to feel safe. Because most who do not know me read me as a cisgender man, I am constantly weighing whether I should come out to my coworkers, feeling the trappings of the closet all over again, trading genuineness for guarded vulnerability, always careful to read others' openness and acceptance towards the LGBTQ+ community.

Recently, a compelling situation confronted me with two options: come out and stand up or stay silent and complicit. The threat of "transphobia," or cissexism, looms large in unstructured social spaces. I brace for instances when people feel the need to voice their negative opinions about transgender people, about whom they know next to nothing apart from inaccurate media portrayals. In the car, headed to an evening of lectures, these thoughts flickered through my mind. Nonetheless, I reassured myself how unlikely it was that the subject of transgender people would come up.

While waiting for the next lecture to start, the subject of conversation went from affirmative action to "You know, the transgender thing has gone too far." My military coworker, a fellow captain, began making comparisons of trans people to transracial people and went further to talk about the unfairness of trans athletes winning competitions. I said, "I'm going to stop you right there. This needs to stay here, but I am trans, and you shouldn't say those things. You don't know who you are sitting next to." Fight or flight response activated with voice firm but shaky, I said, "This is making me emotional because it is personal. And you're wrong about trans athletes. They are not at an unfair advantage." I told my coworkers that trans soldiers are not allowed to serve under the current administration. This was the third time, in a military social setting, that I decided to come out in order to stand up for myself and my community.

I began medical transition in early 2015. Within six months to one year into medical transition, I was consistently perceived as a cisgender man. Being able to pass as cisgender allows me to feel conflicting emotions of gender euphoria and discomfort about being back in the closet. People felt comfortable expressing their negative and ignorant opinions about trans people because they did not know there was a trans person in the room with them. My coming out has been met with both sincere and insincere apologies based on the strength of my relationship with the individuals.

Cissexism had been displayed earlier in the evening when someone pointed out, jokingly, "Do you mean pregnant *wo*man or man?" in response to a story about a pregnant person. Laughter ensued, of course, because nobody was aware that pregnant men do exist and that it is not a joking matter. Or perhaps the punchline was the possibility that men can also be pregnant. The reality is that cissexism is the status quo. It is perpetuated through seemingly harmless jokes such as these, but includes more harmful opinions and, ultimately, the acts of violence committed against transgender people.

What hurts the most is the fact that these negative opinions are held by my coworkers, the patients I treat, and the medical providers I meet. They lay there, just under the surface, waiting to be uncovered. This fact alone is one of the reasons I try to remain "stealth" about my identity. Being seen as "less than" hurts every time, compounding the hurt of years of fighting for survival in a society that punishes difference.

Despite these setbacks, I consider myself one of the more fortunate ones. The timing of the previous ban and the lifting of the ban aligned with my Individual Ready Reserve status as a student, then active duty status, respectively. I was able to receive a gender-affirming and medically necessary surgery in the Army, and there is still the possibility of completing my medical transition, arduous though the process may be in terms of the paperwork and the recovery.

My earnest hope is that we are allowed to serve as authentically as possible. This requires understanding from the newest soldier to the highest strata of leadership. For some, access to medical care—namely medication and/or surgical treatment(s)—can mean life or death or shades in between. For me, being able to complete my medical transition will eliminate my fear of having to use a communal shower in the field or on deployment.

It is comforting to know that I am not alone and simultaneously distressing that each of us must face numerous hurdles to exist in our truest forms. I hope for the day I don't have to live in fear of losing my job for being who I am.

5

Serving with Commitment

We're just like everybody else in the military. We're really just
fighting for the opportunity to serve alongside our brothers
and sisters like everybody else. We're not looking for anything
special.

—Engineman Master Chief Petty Officer (Ret.) Taryn Wilson

Kris Moore, Lieutenant, U.S. Navy, 2005–present

Growing up in Fort Worth, Texas, I often felt out of place, a little weird,
and misunderstood. I didn't fit societal norms of what a little girl should
act like and I felt like everyone had to let me know. "Ladies don't allow
dirt under their fingernails." "Ladies don't wear baseball caps." "Ladies
don't ride around on skateboards." The criticism, which felt more like
taunting, would continue into my late teens and early twenties. I wore
dirty blue jeans, climbed trees, played football, liked to wrestle in the
front yards of friends' houses on hot summer days, those things that
"ladies" didn't do in the early nineties, or so they say. I've never been a
fan of gendering actions, maybe because I was always judged by those
standards and felt constricted by them or, more likely, I learned at a
young age those "standards" were inaccurate and toxic.

Believe it or not, I was a starting offensive tackle on my freshman
football team, the "boys" team. One night, after winning a game, my
mom and I went to dinner. On the way there, mom began crying. I
asked her what was wrong, and she tried to put me off but I knew she
wasn't the emotional type, so I persisted. "One of the moms behind me
said that you and Trey swapped genders . . . ." Trey is my older brother
and was never an athlete, so in the eyes of Southerners he was less than

a man. I can't remember the exact conversation because I was, admittedly, enraged. This woman and her husband had appeared to be very supportive of me, but they broke my mom's heart. I could never forgive that woman for hurting my mom. I could deal with the bullying at school. I could handle being told I was "weird" for doing "manly" things. But what I couldn't handle is seeing my mom in pain because she was second-guessing her actions as a mother.

I've spent the last few years reflecting on what kept me in the closet for so long and every time I come back to that night, a defining event from when I was thirteen. I don't think it's quite that simple, but I do recognize that dramatic events, especially at a young age, can have lifelong impacts. I struggled for years to come to terms with my sexuality and gender identity; I'm thirty-one years old and finally feel comfortable in my own skin.

I witnessed the repeal of "Don't Ask, Don't Tell" as a midshipman, after having served in the closet for just over five years. It was such an elating feeling to be allowed to step out and embrace who I was. A group of my friends and classmates came together to create the first LGBT-ally group at the Naval Academy—Navy Spectrum—in order to have a safe place for LGBT midshipmen and their allies to talk about matters that related to our community. But, in order to be sanctioned by the Naval Academy, we had to take the "T" out of our description and mission statement. At the time, I didn't think it was a big deal; we were still allowed to talk about it and educate people on trans-related matters—who cares if it can't be a part of the name or mission? Years later, I realize how wrong that train of thought was. We pushed on, we invited transgender alumni to come speak to us about their experiences at the Naval Academy, in the fleet, and in the civilian sector. We talked about what it meant to be trans and how there was no single path to transitioning. I began to relate with our speakers and the alumni I would use as mentors more and more. The thought began to creep in the back of my mind "Is this more than empathy? Could I possibly be transgender? Does this explain my childhood? Oh shit."

I was sitting at a bar with my then fiancé in New York City in February 2013, slowly sipping on a beer and clearly lost in thought. We were in NYC to speak to other military academy LGB(T) club leadership to discuss a possible leadership symposium. I had brought up the need to incorporate transgender education into the symposium and in our routine club meetings, but each time I mentioned it I received heavy pushback from two individuals. I was getting annoyed at these meetings, so when we all departed to take a tour of the city my fiancé and I broke off to go grab a drink alone. She asked me if I was okay, asked me what I was thinking about, and then asked me why I was so adamant about pushing for transgender education. I told her it was the right thing to do and we, as a society, will never be okay with something we don't understand, so why not try and understand? She then asked when I was going to come out as transgender. I froze. I hadn't told anyone how I felt, but somehow she knew. I asked her what made her ask such a question. She said that from the look in my eyes and my behavior she could just tell. She told me to embrace who I was and to come out when I was ready, and that she would support whatever decision I made. That was music to my ears. I felt a bit of relief and then a wave of pressure. I felt like it was time and necessary for me to come out, but I had no idea how.

I came out to my parents shortly thereafter and was again met with love and support. They said they would support whatever decision I made and that they just wanted me to be happy but were also concerned for my safety and future in the military. They said, "Just be smart about it, okay?" I knew what they meant was that I had to test the waters before diving into an unknown lake off an unfamiliar dock. Over the next two years I slowly came out to friends, roommates, instructors, mentors, and counselors. I didn't come across a single person who didn't support me for being me. Some didn't quite understand, some may not have believed it was right, but all continued to love and support me.

In May 2014, shortly after graduation, I got married and, despite the ban on transgender service, my wife and I began to talk very seriously about my starting a medical transition. I began by going to a civilian counselor at a nearby LGBT center and, after several months of sessions, she diagnosed me with gender dysphoria. My wife and I agreed that I should start hormone treatments. She even accompanied me to my first appointment with the endocrinologist and gave me my first shot of testosterone. She's not a fan of needles nor hurting people, so I was pleasantly surprised when she had no issues giving me that first injection.

Although I initially thought about waiting to tell my chain of command, I decided to go ahead with it even though I had no idea how the captain would react. Would she be a strict rule-follower and have me processed for discharge? I was incredibly nervous, but I couldn't just give up. I had to trust that she had my back and would at least keep me afloat, if not lead me through the storm, and she did. She said she already had an idea that I was transgender, appreciated me trusting her with this information, and supported whatever decision I made. We agreed that I should come out to the wardroom (officers on the ship) and the Chief's Mess (group of chiefs on the ship) prior to deployment so as to discourage rumors and maintain trust and unity amongst leadership.

The captain called all officers to the wardroom one day for training, as was part of our routine, and gave some updates on things going on around the ship. After she was done with her part, she said, "Ensign Moore has something he wants to say." I don't know what I was expecting her to say but a wave of anxiety hit me like a ton of bricks. My heart was racing, I was visibly sweating, and I wasn't sure I'd be able to speak. I stood up and started off with, "Thank you ma'am. Does everyone know what transgender means?" The captain broke in, "KMoore"—my nickname—"they don't live under a rock, get on with it!" I must admit, this didn't help the nerves a bit, but I did as I was told. "Well, I'm transgender. I was born in a female body, was raised as a girl, but have never felt right about it. I've recently began taking hormones to transition to living as a man. I just wanted to let all of you know because you will be seeing and hearing changes soon and I don't want there to be a bunch of rumors floating around. If you'd like to tell your divisions, or have me tell your divisions, I'm good with that. But I just don't want rumors getting in the way of our jobs." I stopped speaking, pretty abruptly, so there was a look of waiting on everyone's faces. "Does anyone have any questions for me?" "Are you happy!?" I heard my chief engineer speak up, her voice was loud and caught me off guard. I couldn't tell if she was asking me a legitimate question or if it was meant in a negative way, so I asked, "I'm sorry?" "Are you happy?" She said it more questioning and calm this time. "Is"—insert wife's name here—"happy?" I told her, "Yes, I am and I believe she is as well." "Then who gives a shit what anyone else thinks?" I wanted to cry. I wasn't expecting to get my ass kicked, but I definitely wasn't expecting such aggressive support either. A huge weight was lifted off my shoulders and I started to feel free, like I could really focus on my work now. As we were dismissed, every single person in that wardroom came up and either shook my hand, told me how proud they were of me, hugged me, or some combination of them all. I had to go to my room to gather myself. I wasn't expecting to be so emotionally drained after that.

I continued hormone treatment through deployment, began to use men's restrooms overseas (because I could no longer safely get away with using the women's restrooms), and started living as a male. It was such an amazing feeling to experience this sort of liberty for the first time. When I was on my way home from deployment, I received word that the trans ban had been lifted. Once I had followed the required, but yet to be determined, process, I would be able to change my name and gender marker. Almost immediately, I began scheduling the necessary appointments. Most challenging of all was understanding the required protocol for getting it all done. I asked a lot of questions and tried to be nice to the people who helped me, so for the most part I had a pretty easy time with my paperwork and appointments.

One day in July 2017, having been out at sea for a brief period of time, my ship returned to port. I was sitting down in the wardroom, eating lunch, when I heard on the 1MC (general announcing system), "Lieutenant Junior Grade Moore, your presence is requested in the commanding officer's cabin." I'll clue you in on a little secret: a junior officer being chimed to the captain's cabin during lunch is never a good thing. Usually, our next ranking person (department head, a lieutenant) would be called first, not us. I thought maybe it was something about sea and anchor detail or some other bridge watch–related thing, but then I saw my command master chief (CMC) in there as well, and when she turned to look at me my world slowly turned dark. "Come on in, Kris, have a seat." My tension grew because my commanding officer hardly ever talked to me so gently, and why was my CMC here anyway; who died? "Have you seen the news today?" "No, sir, I don't typically watch the news on the ship. Is everything okay?" My mind immediately searched for clues— was there a mass shooting where my family lives, did something happen in Norfolk and my wife was involved? What the hell is going on!? My captain turned the volume up on his TV and I immediately saw the scroll with something along the lines of "Trump to ban transgender service members from serving in military." I felt the blood drain from my face, my hands went numb, and I remember having trouble hearing anything other than the loud tone in my ear like an audiogram gone bad. I remember hearing my CMC ask me multiple times if I was okay, but I couldn't answer. Not that I didn't want to say something, I just couldn't get words to come out. I was on this merry-go-round from hell and I couldn't figure out how to get sound to come out of me. My captain looked me in the eyes and told me, "Nothing changes, tweets aren't policy, and this won't last. There's no way this can be legal. We will continue to support you and you will continue to do your job." I know those were exactly the words I wanted to hear, but I couldn't process it quite yet. I could feel myself begin to cry, something I hadn't done since starting testosterone almost two years prior, so I asked if I could be excused. "I want you to take the rest of the day off, Kris. Go home." "Sir, I really don't want to be alone right now." He understood and told me I could work out of my stateroom for as long as I needed and to let him know if he could do anything for me. I went to my stateroom and immediately lost control of every emotion surging through my body. I ugly cried. My roommate walked in and I didn't even try to hide it, not that it was even possible at this point. He grabbed my shoulders and asked what happened. I turned on the news and he just hugged me. He held me until I patted him on the back and said thank you. At this time, I was smoking, so I went outside to the smoke deck and quickly realized the entire ship had seen the news. I should have known; all the TVs are on during lunch and word gets around a ship faster than you'd imagine. The chiefs that were out there immediately noticed me and recognized my pain. They created a circle around me so the younger sailors couldn't see me when I began to cry again and then someone asked me, "Sir, what does this mean for you?" I wanted to yell, "The fuck if I know!" But I just said, "Nothing. Tweets aren't policy. Nothing changes." Everyone out there knew I was full of shit, but what else was there to say?

I had a mastectomy consult the following Monday up in Bethesda, a five-hour drive from Norfolk. I had arranged to be relieved from duty a few hours early so I could make it up there in time for my appointment. When I finally got in to see the surgeon, I was told, "I just got back from leave and haven't even read your file, have you started testosterone?" Given that I now had chest hair, a "five-o'clock shadow" from not having yet shaved that morning, and a deep voice, I was a little annoyed by his question but tried to remain calm. "Yes, I've been on testosterone for nearly two years, sir." "Oh, okay, well given the recent policy change, I can't see you for top surgery, but we can do imaging and other tests just in case this all blows over." "Sir, no policy has been released, those were tweets." "Yes, but I've been ordered not to continue gender-transition-related care until further notice." At this point I was pissed off and hurt. When I reported back to my ship the next day, I immediately went to my doctor and captain about what I could do. As much as they disagreed with the surgeon, we agreed there wasn't much anyone could do until some sort of clarifying orders came out. As of this writing, it's now been almost two years and, after several more consults, I am still waiting for a surgery date.

There are people out there that will argue having transgender service members in our nation's military only brings disorder and disrupts unit cohesion. I've been in the Navy for thirteen years now, four of which have been as a transgender officer. I come to work every day to do the job, to mentor midshipmen, to teach classes, and coach rugby players. I strive to be the best I can be, to help promote team unity, and accomplish our mission. I'm a sailor first. I just happen to be transgender.

Blake Dremann, Lieutenant Commander, U.S. Navy, 2005–present

In the course of a year and a half, I hit three big, historic milestones. In 2010, I completed a shipboard assignment in Japan, was headed to Afghanistan, and I had just quietly come out as a lesbian. "Don't Ask, Don't Tell" was still a year from repeal. By the time I showed up in Afghanistan, I hadn't even finished telling my friends and family. When you're in Afghanistan, there are only three things you do: you're either working, reading, or working out. I'm not big on the gym, so there was a lot of reading.

I ordered every gender and sexuality book on Amazon that I could because, after all, I'm a Bible college kid. There I was, going on thirty, and I didn't know any of this stuff. My upbringing hadn't prepared me for this, and I was just discovering what all this kind of meant for me. I read Leslie Feinberg's *Stone Butch Blues* and I so identified with the character that I was bawling while reading. I just figured that I was a butch lesbian but, while reading, two things happened. One, I discovered the word "transgender" and started to explore what that meant for me. Second, in January 2011, someone pointed me to an online group that asked, "Do you identify as transgender?" To be a member, the answer had to be yes. The more I thought about it, I said to myself, "You know what? Yeah, I do."

No sooner did I realize that I was transgender, when I found myself being selected as the first woman to be on a submarine. There I was, about to be famous and a part of naval history for being a female, but I'm really a man. I had no idea how I was going to handle that. My first challenge was a seven-month training pipeline. There were several times during the course of training where senior leaders would sit down with all of the female submariners and convey confusion as to why I was there. The primary difference between me now and what I looked like in 2011 is that I had more hair then. Not much more hair, but more. I had the stocky build, and people had trouble remembering that I was a female.

I chose my name while I was in my first six weeks of class, and I still hadn't really told anybody that I was trans. I came out to the first person in the Navy about two or three months later. She was someone I felt safe with; she was going through the pipeline with me and we had become good friends. She was like, "Oh, cool, this is awesome." So she's always called me B or Blake; B as a cover and Blake when we were in private.

Submarine life was difficult to adjust to on top of figuring out my identity and how being trans was going to work. I was the first of my kind to show up on the boat, and now I've got to figure out how to be a submariner. It was not an easy task, particularly for someone who doesn't like math. Over the course of eighteen months, while working the mental math and learning about nuclear strategy, I managed to think through the idea that my gender needed to change.

By December 2012, I'd been deployed for five years straight and I was struggling with burnout. I was constantly coming and going, and I started to break. The problem was that I was on a nuclear weapons submarine. Going to see a military doctor about mental health issues could have put my position in jeopardy. Luckily, as an officer, I have the privilege that when I say I have a doctor's appointment, I'm allowed to go without having to be specific about what doctor I'm going to see. I found myself a therapist in Seattle and started seeing her when I was in port. Unfortunately, that was difficult because I spent most of 2013 at sea.

We deployed twice that year, so my therapist appointments were probably further apart than I'd have liked, but it calmed me down to the point of being able to function through my next deployment, which was the worst patrol ever. We had three inspections, two of which we did not do well on. At the same time, the captain was trying to make me a more well-rounded submariner and put me into a position in which I was not very good. He kept expecting me to get better, but it wasn't happening and my stress level rose.

They left me on the submarine for forty-two months. That isn't typical; the problem was that I had to be relieved by a female. Because gender integration was so new, they were still keeping some jobs labeled as male and female until we had "grown" more senior nuclear-qualified females. The supply officer had to be the most senior female on the boat. By that time, the luster of being the first woman in submarines had worn off and you couldn't just pull any female into the seven-month pipeline.

Up to then, I'd been very cautious about starting a medical transition. My biggest fears were embarrassing my family and embarrassing the Navy by being found out. Because if I'm found out while still on the submarine, it's big news. My social life was almost nonexistent other than hanging out with some of the girls that I went through training with and kind of knew. I didn't know how long I would be able to handle it. But I figured that if it was going to change I had to stay.

In October of 2013, I had a conversation with a friend who was undergoing his own medical transition. We'd served together on our first ship and he was the one that convinced me to come out of the closet. I asked him, "How are you doing? How are you getting away with taking hormones on the ship?" He said, "I just keep them in my room." The entire reason that I started hormones then was because he told me they didn't need to be refrigerated. Though I controlled the fridge on the boat, I thought that my going there to grab some little plastic bag of my own that I'm keeping in there would look kind of suspicious. My next question was, "How do I make this happen?"

I got a referral to the Seattle LGBT clinic, but I just told my boss, "I got an appointment and I need to go to Seattle." I met with the doctor there and she actually told me she wasn't going to prescribe me hormones for two reasons. First, I was two weeks from getting underway for another seventy-five days. Second, because I wasn't going to tell the military. I was really upset after that appointment and thought transition just wasn't in the cards for me. At least not right then.

I went back to my therapist and I was really upset. I hadn't done anything transition-wise other than identify, pick a name, and live as male in my nonmilitary time, which was rare. She sent me to a different clinic. They were more than happy to get me started on a low dose of testosterone. They took my blood, did some blood tests, and I came back a week later to sign all my informed-consent letters. They shipped hormones to my house, I took my first shot, and I got underway five days later. On the boat, I had to figure out how I was going to do this on a regular basis. Luckily only officers use our head [bathroom] and it's often empty. I'd go in and take my shot at one or two in the morning.

In March of 2014, on the basis of back problems, I got a full double mastectomy. The doctor called it the man boob surgery where guys that lost weight had extra skin removed. We were in an extended yard period, so I didn't have to be on the boat and I was allowed to take a full two weeks of leave. I managed all this in the middle of what felt like a witch hunt. We had more people discharged for being transgender in 2014 than we did any other year. In SPARTA alone, we saw ten to twelve of roughly two hundred members discharged on this basis.

I thought I was keeping it all under wraps and didn't think anybody on the boat knew. I probably could have kept it that way. However, it turned out that I had a sailor who was trans and was getting out of the military because she needed to transition. We weren't in a position where the policy was changing yet, but she wasn't shy about the fact that she was transitioning. Her being so open about it made the crew suspect me. It was no secret that I had gone and had surgery and looked and acted like a guy. My voice had changed, but I'm also a smoker. I figured everybody thought that was part of it.

I found out later from my captain that the executive officer had suspected that I was trans. Two reasons kept them from saying anything. One, I was good at my job, and two, there was nobody to replace me. Do you report that your supply officer is trans and settle for just not having one? Or do you overlook this little fact when it's not affecting their ability to do job and just let that be. I did another year on the boat, completing a fifth patrol. I had been deployed for seven of eight years. I was tired.

They finally let me leave in April of 2015 and I was assigned to a job in the Pentagon. They had been waiting on me for two years. I had been selected for the position in May of 2013, but because it was an internship there was nobody I was relieving so the position remained available. I ended up being quite senior for the position and my coworkers were looking at me funny, and all I could think was, "Goddamn submarines."

Three months after I left the submarine, I was selected for promotion to lieutenant commander. Three weeks later, I was announced as the Vice Admiral Batchelder winner, which is the top logistics award for the Navy. If I hadn't been extended for that second time, I would never have submitted the package for consideration. The time of the award goes from November of 2013 to November 2014. This was exactly when I started my medical transition. It was the time I started to gain some personal confidence and recharged. I had been able to discover my identity and was still the best at what I did.

During the internship I wasn't able to hide my identity. In just three days I was found out. It was because that was the first time I'd ever worked for female officers. One asked me if I went by a different name outside of work. I told her, "Yeah, I use Blake. I'm working on getting legally changed." I left for the day and she called me an hour later, saying, "We've discussed it, and if you're okay with it, we'd like to start using Blake like a call sign"—a call sign being, among other things, a military nickname. There was no big announcement; from then on, everybody just assumed my name was Blake and that I was male like it was no big thing.

This took place right after Carter made the announcement that they were going to put a moratorium on the discharges and study changing the policy on transgender personnel. I became a very convenient spokesperson to senior military leaders because I was in the building and had such a strong record. Take the shyest guy in the room and stick them in front of a bunch of four-star generals and admirals? Not what I really wanted, but it sure paid off when open service was announced.

What I want people to know is that we continue to serve with honor and dignity. First and foremost, despite all the BS, I still want to be here. Despite the fact I know there are people I work with who would love to see transgender people kicked out of the military, for no other reason than that they don't like them. Women, African Americans, gays, and lesbians have been treated like shit since they started integrating into the regular forces, yet they continue to volunteer to serve; so do trans people. I continue to serve. I am qualified to serve. I don't need a welcome mat; I just need everyone to do their job like they expect me to do mine.

Allison Caputo, Captain, U.S. Coast Guard, 1995–present

I am an active duty captain in the United States Coast Guard. I have always loved the ocean; my mom says I was born with sand in my toes. I grew up on the sandy beaches of Long Island, New York, and, having developed a love for nature and the environment, I joined the Coast Guard. As a result of this, I have traveled around the world, to the Caribbean, Central and South America, Europe, Russia, China, and the South Pacific. I have been on five cutters with eleven years of sea time and commanded the Coast Guard cutter *Campbell*. I have negotiated treaties and fostered international law enforcement cooperation. I have stopped drug smugglers and seized illegal fishing vessels on the high seas. And I also have gender dysphoria and identify as a trans woman.

I knew something was not right from an early age, but I didn't have the words for it. Why do others wear the dresses, have long hair, and attend tea parties? I quickly understood I was a boy and was expected to conform to the "boy" expectations put before me. I ran away from home when I was just four years old, but my neighbors promptly returned me. The world didn't make sense to me and I struggled to fit in. I got through high school working on the yearbook, bowling, and serving both as team mascot and on the prom committee. Of course, I liked to be with girls, but mostly I wanted to be *like* them, which was confusing. Joining the military seemed like a way to allow me to meet everyone's expectations.

I went to the Coast Guard Academy in 1991. I was seventeen years old at the time and it was not an easy experience. I almost didn't make it through the training of swab summer, because I had difficulty conforming. I was brought down to the military medical doctors so that they could evaluate me. Puberty sucked and I was in the middle of mine. I thought, well, if they do some psychological exam or find something wrong with me, at least I tried. They concluded that I had a bad self-image because I had acne. I was treated for this affliction and continued with the training, but I resolved myself never to be called to medical again. I joined the crew team because they were the toughest bastards on campus. I decided this would keep me out of the barracks and away from trouble. I certainly enjoyed my marine science studies but spent my academy years barely surviving. At the end, I received my bachelor's degree and my commission and I was soon off to Alaska to experience raw nature and to save the fish!

During my service, I continued to struggle with my gender identity. Over time, things continued to get worse so I buried my feelings very deeply, like in a chest with chains and steel locks at the bottom of the ocean. During the line-crossing ceremony, an initiation rite that celebrates one's first crossing of the equator, I was chosen to be King Neptune's wife, Queen Amphitrite. I didn't really mind this that much at all; in fact, I enjoyed it. But it was a cruel irony that I should enjoy something meant to be embarrassing.

To make myself feel better about my gender, I did things like purchase model kits for the paint they contained and use it as toenail polish. When my roommate was away, I would put socks in my shirt to simulate breasts. I didn't talk with anybody about these feelings, not even a chaplain, for fear of being found out and discharged. And the fear was not unfounded, as the "Don't Ask, Don't Tell" policy would potentially label me as "gay" and target me for discharge.

I got married to a friend from high school, thinking it could make me conform to the "appropriate" gender role. I think it had the opposite effect. The Halloween after getting married we cross-dressed, and I of course thoroughly enjoyed being in a dress and makeup. I confessed to my wife I would rather be like this but that I didn't think people would understand. She was obviously upset and took an approach of "do what you need to do," so I would cross-dress in private to make myself feel better. Of course, after a while, I was assigned to a new ship and felt the need to display that I could be tough and stern. I got rid of my women's clothing and prepared to be the best department head possible for the cutter. I shaved my head again and took on a hard persona, trying to reinvent myself. This was both gut-wrenching and counterproductive. I didn't do well and made a lot of mistakes, but I think I was too focused on trying to embody the strong male archetype. It made me weep sometimes and I hated myself, but I thought that was what everyone wanted me to be.

I continued to go to sea and I enjoyed it. When you are deployed, the problems of land seem to go away. You focus on your job; it becomes the great equalizer where everyone is the same and gendered things don't tend to matter as much. Unfortunately, this took a toll on my marriage and it was difficult for me to be away from my kids. Being ashore was difficult as my desire to be female would assert itself. I would play video games because if I couldn't be a female in the real world I could at least be one in the virtual world. In the real world sometimes, my duties would make me cry because I didn't like who I was, but I felt there was nothing I could do about it. Eventually, I found that my female persona could not be held back. Many times, as executive officer, I was told I was too nice or that I needed to yell at people or that I wasn't hard enough. I just explained that this was not my way. I would be myself and care for people, I would give out treats, and if that wasn't good enough then so be it because I couldn't be somebody I wasn't.

My life changed when, after being married for twenty years, my wife said she wanted a divorce. I was devastated, and I blamed myself. No matter how hard I tried, I couldn't be the husband my wife desired. I was going to end my life rather than face the social stigma of coming out. It was all quite simple; I would get in my truck and drive off the bridge into the sea. They say when you are in crisis everything goes black and you don't think any more, you just do what you were trained to do. As an executive officer, I had advised many people to call the employee assistance program (EAP), so I literally heard myself say to myself, "What are you doing? Call EAP!" So I got some help through a Coast Guard support hotline. I was given a civilian counselor and from about May through October we talked about my marriage and my gender issues. When I finally went to Coast Guard medical, I carried a note that stated my issues. I almost didn't give it to the physician assistant, but I knew things would not get better, so with tears in my eyes and trembling I handed her the note. I couldn't even look at her, fearing the reaction. She took her time and said, "Thank you for sharing. Can I get somebody who knows about this to help you?" I barely squeaked out a "yes" as I nodded.

The doctor came in and said he could help me because he had attended a seminar on trans health care and also worked at Walter Reed National Military Medical Center. I was referred to Walter Reed, received a diagnosis for gender dysphoria, and began treatment in November 2016. At that time there was not yet a formal policy, just a message about allowing trans military members to serve. I joined a support group that had only been meeting since August. Clearly, transitioning was in my future as a way to ease my discomfort. However, like anything else, I had lots of doubts: Would people accept me? Would I even survive the process? The support group was very helpful; trans persons are extremely vulnerable and having people to talk with is critical to their survival. The Coast Guard manual for military transgender service came out in December 2016. I read it and submitted my transition plan, a plan that required me to make too many unnecessary compromises, such as when

I could begin hormone replacement therapy (HRT). Per the military, I couldn't start HRT until my plan was approved and since I was a senior officer my plan was sent up and down the chain of command, which took a very long time.

In the end, my command denied me exceptions to policy (ETP), nor would they allow me to pursue real-life experience (RLE), stating that I must adhere to the uniform and grooming standards and facilities consistent with my current gender marker (male). The admiral also wanted to review all policies and procedures before making any decisions, which meant that I couldn't have HRT, ETPs, or RLE. I wasn't sure how any of this was going to work. In April, however, endocrinology contacted me and gave me my HRT pills. This, however, created a dilemma. Medical had prescribed HRT meds for my condition, but the administration forbade me to take it. When I was finally able to begin HRT, I immediately began to feel better. Finally, in mid-June, I received my paperwork from personnel support command (PSC) granting approval to transition, with all my ETPs dated June 1, 2017.

The day I received my transition paperwork, a coworker I had known since the academy asked to speak with me privately. He informed me that my hair was out of regulation. I had pretty much decided that my last haircut was going to be in May and had forgotten to keep up with it. I handed him the folder with my transition letter in it. He looked at the memo, reading it very slowly. Then he looked at me. Then he read it a second time. Then he responded, "So you have a chit [note granting permission] for your hair," and proceeded to walk out. I stopped him and said, "Wait, I need your assistance. How do we tell everybody in an orderly fashion?" We decided that I would have a prepared statement for the Maritime Law Enforcement section, the people I worked with directly, so I could answer any questions. I would also send prepared statements to other office chiefs so that they could inform their staff. I was set to implement the plan on July 8, 2017. The reaction was truly supportive. The first day was really hard, but it got better each and every day after that. I could never envision ever going back.

Just over two weeks later, the president stated that trans members could no longer serve and I was disappointed and depressed. I got the call from PSC saying that they were not sure what the tweet meant, but that nothing had changed, the current policy remained in place, and to keep working until we figured this out. My response was to ask how the others were doing and if anyone had called them. At the time, there were only thirteen trans service members in the Coast Guard, and I believed they were at risk for self-harm. They informed me they had made contact with everyone and that I had been the last. "Well," I said, "it is my pleasure to serve and I will continue to do so until told otherwise." Unfortunately, one of my trans coworkers tried to take her life but, fortunately, was stopped and wound up at Walter Reed for a time. I was very proud when the commandant of the Coast Guard stated he was committed to continued trans service and would not "break faith" with us. I had sailed with him on Coast Guard cutter *Rush* and I knew the type of character he had, but to put his career on the line to defend the small group of us was unbelievably noble. Truly, the Coast Guard is my family. I cannot thank them enough for their support in my darkest hours.

Having been promoted to captain, I knew I would be transferred, so I would need to complete my transition before leaving for a new duty station. It was time to address gender reassignment surgery (GRS), but, once again the administration began throwing doubts into my plan. I worried, for example, "What if I can't get it done in time?" There were concerns about recovery time and the risks, requiring me to make an amendment to my treatment plan, which involved again the embarrassing process of explaining GRS to my supervisors. Because, as a result of the tweets, surgeries were on hold, I decided to do this on my own. I obtained the name of a reputable surgeon in New Hope, Pennsylvania, which wasn't too far away. Turns out she was prior military *and* transgender! I contacted her office and was able to get an appointment. She said that she could perform the GRS in April, provided that I had completed one year on HRT, *and* that she would do the work pro bono with my just needing to pay the hospital fees. I made the arrangements myself.

Of course, PSC was not too happy with me, but I said, "Aren't I just following my approved plan, even if the government is not supporting me?" They said I was pursuing elective surgery, and I said, "No, it is not. This is required for my transition as stated in my revised plan, and you approved it." In the end we arrived at a compromise under a rare miscellaneous section of the manual whereby I could have the convalescence leave but I had to sign my rights away, i.e., were anything to happen to me in surgery, the government wouldn't cover me. It was very scary.

My support group during GRS was composed of friends and shipmates. My family was not in a position or of a mind to help or understand me. Quite the opposite. I felt if I told them, they would try to stop me as they hadn't taken my coming out very well. I had a team: a former commanding officer, a spouse of a former commanding officer, a classmate from the academy, and an officer in the National Oceanic and Atmospheric Administration who was also trans. These people graciously supported me by taking turns assisting me on different days. I can never thank them enough for their kindness. After four weeks of recovery, I filed for my gender marker change and it was officially completed on June 1, 2018, one year after I had begun my transition. I was transferred a month later, driving over four thousand miles to Juneau, Alaska. As of this writing, I serve as the chief of law enforcement for 3.8 million square miles of ocean, working directly with interagency partners and international partners to stop illegal fishing, protecting a six-billion-dollar industry.

I wake up every day just happy to be me, but I know others are suffering and it isn't fair. While I feel content, I know people who are struggling with gender identity. Unfortunately, the new policy makes trans persons unable to serve as themselves. It forces a cruel choice, present as the gender on your birth certificate or get out. It treats you as a person with an incurable disease, which they will not treat, but with which they will let you suffer. You are essentially a second-class citizen who will be disciplined if you do not conform to the gender with which you don't identify. I often find it challenging to face the reality that while the Coast

Guard accepts me for who I am, my current government that I serve and protect does not, though I do have hope that things can change and that there is the potential that people can accept us for who we are.

Eve, Petty Officer First Class, U.S. Navy, 2004—present

Reluctantly, and at the behest of my spouse who had painfully watched my emotional decline over the course of a few years, I began my transition early in the winter of 2016. We had been married for a decade and they had seen all the signs. After a rather sudden suicide attempt that landed me in the inpatient ward at the regional military medical hospital, they realized the conflict that was going on in my head. They knew that my transition was necessary. Even when the new military policy had gone live and open service became allowed, I had denied it. They told me they would more appreciate a living, thriving wife than a dead, or at best, a chronically and morbidly depressed husband.

During the late spring of 2017, I spent a few months in a school for advanced signals analysts. I wasn't particularly "out" out, but if I suspected that someone might be an ally, I wouldn't hide who I was. By that personal rule, I became fairly good friends with two others at the school. Part-time, outside of classes, I lived as Eve. I didn't have an exception to policy at the time. I'd requested one from my commanding officer because the wonderful side effects of estrogen had begun and breast development was booming. Daily, I was conducting physical training (PT) with many "pipeliners," trainees who have just completed boot camp. It was getting difficult to do PT without binding my chest, which can be dangerous for a number of reasons ranging from skin issues like scarring and infection to respiratory issues. I was also starting to look very androgynous. It was time to switch regulations. I needed to be following the guidelines for women. My request was denied.

In the eyes of my commanding officer (CO), I was in a prime position to teach all these junior service members about the policy. They made a stand for me and told me that if either instructors or students had an issue with me wearing a sports bra as part of my PT gear, that they could come speak with them personally. I was a little miffed by this, but to have that surprise backing from them told me a lot about this CO. They immediately had my respect on a personal level. However, the apprehensive feeling of not being able to wholly appear as I should lingered.

For the duration of my time at this school, every other weekend I was making road trips to where my family lived. I had relocated them to where my new command would be, so they could establish daily life there and enroll our oldest child in school and have him placed in the care of a therapist. At the beginning of July 2017, for one of those weekends, I opted to not make the drive back. The stresses of school were wearing on me and the added stress of a long drive wasn't what I needed. I decided to remain near the school and rest.

I didn't always go out presenting as a woman, but I'd been starting to feel better and better about my appearance and skills at blending in. One weekend that July, I was assaulted outside my hotel, in slowly fading, but still broad daylight. I have no doubt that I was assaulted for being who I was, a transgender woman. The hotel's manager pushed the assailants off of me and called the police. A friend to whom I was out as trans took me to the emergency room. A few hours later, I was released. Fortunately, I had "only" three bruised ribs and a cranial contusion.

Ultimately, this was a significant turning point in my life. It led to me leaving the transgender community at large, drastically condensing my social circles. I realized then that there are *many* people in this country that didn't understand, appreciate, or support my existence. Weeks later, in late July 2017, the tweets of my commander in chief would reinforce that notion. Ultimately, I would succumb to the shame that many transgender people suffer, but I would remain open. I would remain proud. I *wanted* people to see me as a strong service member, as a strong leader. I wanted my tenure to be recognized and upheld.

Suddenly, I found that my continued service was under so much scrutiny that my current medical team deemed me unfit to move on to my new command—a tactical unit with a deployment scheduled within the next year. I was rescreened for suitability. That screening was conducted under a microscope and forcibly redone. Twice. Ultimately, nobody could find any reason why a transitioning woman *couldn't* serve in a deploying unit. A week after graduation from the Signal School, I was released from medical hold and sent to my new command.

The following months at my new command were fairly bumpy. Within two weeks of my arrival, knowledge of my identity and transition had become common knowledge. I was the talk of the unit. Many supporters reached out to me on social media and were fairly protective of me. Opposition took bits and pieces of the same so they could have a laugh at me among themselves. It was always easy to tell who took particular offense to my presence. Ironically, the senior enlisted member at the unit had recently told all members at the command, during mandated transgender policy training, that this sort of thing would *never* happen. A biological male would never be able to come to a tactical unit and switch gender markers, never be able to come live in female accommodations. I was met with *great* opposition by the senior enlisted and commissioned members within the command. At one point, my CO even took steps to try and stop my active transition, which was obviously impossible since they had already accepted my medical screening.

I served almost one year with that unit. Almost.

I'd been with the unit long enough that I eventually grew comfortable with them and thought I knew on whom I could and could not rely. After great effort, I had successfully changed my gender marker to read female. I had begun following the appropriate regulations and begun living in the appropriate quarters. For a change, life was going my way. I was a prominent figure with the equal opportunity committee; the regional up-echelon flag officer knew me by virtue of the work I was doing for my community and service as a whole. My breaking point came after an assault by a senior enlisted member in whom I'd placed an undue amount of trust. I was singled out for what I was. I reported it, and it was suggested by my command that I leave the unit for my own safety. I agreed, and I was placed again in a medical hold status while the investigation took its course. It took nearly a year for the investigation to be completed.

Before I was transferred to the unit I currently find myself in, a couple of close friends I'd made within SPARTA suggested that I attempt to go "stealth." That is, try my hand at hiding in plain sight. At first, I was very skeptical about the idea. I'd laughingly said I'd do it the moment it presented itself, but doing so in the military presents a LOT of issues.

I'll be the first to acknowledge that genetics were very kind to me. Physically, I'm indistinguishable from most other women. I know not everybody in this fluctuating community is a believer in what some refer to as the "privilege of passing." Whether or not it exists is beyond me, but being able to hide in plain sight is very much based on one's ability to do just that.

The question is . . . how does one hide being transgender in a culture that has that status fresh on its mind? As a force, we recently underwent the ordered acceptance of our kind, mandated training, then the attempted order at removing acceptance of us and our service with it. Every transfer screening I would ever face would be marred by a screaming F64.1 code, denoting that I suffered from gender dysphoria.

I reported to my new unit after having had only one interaction with them beforehand. A friend with whom I'd served over a decade was also stationed here. They were supportive of me the entire time and wholeheartedly agreed to help me maintain my cover story. It's a small detachment of a training command of ten service members—all closely knit, all very, very kind and caring. I'll admit that it may have been a little simpler to hide in when it's such a small, family-like unit with an even male-to-female split. I only incurred suspicion when an attempt was made to secure a new logon for the local network. My DoD ID number was still associated with my former name and was never updated, as the system didn't mirror DEERS. It was easy to feign ignorance as to why that would be happening. Upon reporting to the unit, I had to undergo my first urinalysis exam. My friend volunteered to come proctor for me so as to keep things as quiet as possible, much to my glee. I was elated to not have to explain anything to the processing division.

My new unit agreed to send me to school to become an instructor. They were under no obligation to do so, knowing that I wasn't there as a permanent body, due to the nature of a medical hold. It was mutually decided that I would do so, as it would potentially provide great benefit. There were a good number of schools scheduled for the next few months and few instructors qualified to teach them. Over the course of nearly twelve weeks of instructing, only one member with whom I'd previously served enrolled as a student. After two weeks, they finally realized who I was and ultimately chose to ignore that interaction and treat me like someone they had never known, for better or worse. To say that interaction didn't eat at me would be an utter lie; the climate of the military and the country have conditioned me to feel as though my survival literally rests on my ability to remain hidden.

Recently, while writing this essay, I underwent sex reassignment surgery. In order to undergo the procedure, I was required to obtain the approval of the top officer at my unit. Their education regarding my situation had come a couple months prior, when they had to chair a development board that assessed my continued service and professional growth. They were the only member to notice that my previous fitness reports were all written for a male. We spoke privately about it, and they were *very* understanding about my concerns of privacy and my preference to remain under the radar, as it were.

A month after my surgery, I returned to duty. I taught my first class six weeks post-operative. Nobody could tell anything had changed, as was intended by design. Recovery was fast and relatively painless. I was able to maintain the maintenance schedule as was required by my surgeon without any negative impact on my unit. Three months post-operative, I found myself suddenly being reassigned. I was directed to return to a tactical unit in a new location, given barely over one month to ready myself and my family for the move. In preparation for doing so, I had a sit-down with my medical care team to see what we could do regarding invisibility. They are the members most educated in these matters, obviously, but I've been a catalyst to a lot of their growth.

When I was about to transfer, I discussed the coding of my medical record with my doctors to try and update it to a more modern standard. However, instead of updating the code, they removed it. Now, medical providers can look back on my previous treatments, but ongoing treatment for gender dysphoria isn't annotated in the forefront of my record. As I've fully completed my medical treatment plan, I am no longer required to ask my CO to approve its continuation, nor do they need to know that I was even treated for gender dysphoria. Assuming somebody at my gaining unit doesn't have insider information otherwise, I don't expect that anyone at the unit will have any clue that I transitioned.

This doesn't stop the constant fear that someone at my gaining command will find cause to delve into the depths of my service record for more information about me, coming up with more information than I had planned to divulge. Being that my transition began and ended within the past five years, there will always be a relatively high chance that someone could inadvertently uncover my identity while looking for unrelated information regarding my performance history. Flaws exist with the distinctly gendered language which we use to write our performance evaluations. We are able to submit corrections to only the administratively identifying portions of these reports. Even then, in the filed record, the reports themselves aren't changed; they merely append the changes in shorthand memorandum, drawing more attention to the report on record.

After months of fighting it, I've conceded to the fact that my ability to keep my past quiet rests solely on what brought me this far in my transition on active duty—dumb luck and the kindness of others. I can't realistically expect that my former life would just be swept under the rug and that nobody from my past wouldn't ever recognize me. I can merely hope that when that good fortune doesn't smile on me, the acceptance shown by my senior officers will lead others to overlook a past to which the Trump administration has assigned a shameful scarlet letter.

If ever the day comes that it's proven to me that this is all just a futile game of hide and seek, I'll abdicate my ill-conceived notion of camouflage. Until then, I intend to use every protection (true or purported) this so-called stealth will afford myself and my family.

Molly T. Sackman, Petty Officer First Class, U.S. Navy, 2006–present

As of this writing, I have completed over twelve years of service. I currently serve as a petty officer first class onboard the USS *Wayne E. Meyer*, a destroyer out of Pearl Harbor, Hawaii. My rate (career field) is that of an AEGIS fire controlman, which means I work on the AEGIS weapon system which protects ships from inbound threats. My career has been pretty standard. I do my job and I do it well. Being a sailor is an integral part of who I am. It has taken me to countries I never imagined visiting. And it has given me a sense of pride and accomplishment. As a transgender woman, the Navy has been a blessing and a burden. My journey has been convoluted and confusing, made even more so by my naval service. But every story has a beginning and this is mine.

In 2012, I told my fiancée, Crystal, I wanted to try on women's clothing. I don't why. I had never wanted to before; it just seemed like a good idea at the time. I had just come off of a rough nine-month deployment that included events like my dad passing away and a shipmate committing suicide weeks before pulling into our homeport. Maybe something inside me broke or jumbled loose. Whatever the reason, it just felt like something I had to do. Crystal, being the ever-loving and supportive woman she is, said, "Sure!" The next weekend we headed to Hillcrest, an LGBT district in San Diego. With a visit to a very friendly thrift shop and after some apprehensive moments, I found myself dressed as a girl. Even without fully feminizing my features, it felt right! I had anticipated feeling uncomfortable or maybe even repulsed, but things just clicked into place. I knew that under the Uniform Code of Military Justice I could be punished or lose my career for "cross-dressing," not to mention the harassment I could receive from my shipmates, but there was no turning back. In the weeks that followed, I acquired a bra with false breasts, an array of makeup to hide my beard shadow, and a growing closet of women's clothing. I also had a name for my new alter ego—Molly. I had plucked the name rather haphazardly from *The Dresden Files*, a fantasy book series. Had I known back then how this would develop, I may have put more thought into it! As it stands now, it's my legal name.

I was living in an on-base apartment but couldn't risk leaving base as "Molly," so I changed at a shop in Northpark, another LGBT neighborhood in San Diego. Crystal always did my makeup, and once I was dressed and ready to go we would hit up bars and restaurants in Hillcrest and Northpark. It was thrilling, and expressing my feminine side gave me a wonderful sense of freedom. I also delved into books and researched my cross-dressing. During my inquiry I found a label that seemed to fit—genderfluid. It explained that a person's gender identity could float between male and female. I latched onto this since it allowed Joshua and Molly to coexist.

When I finally moved off base, I was still terrified of being seen by fellow sailors and avoided malls, theaters, and other popular spots, restricting myself to the LGBT areas. But it was becoming a bit repetitive simply going to the same places over and over again, so for a change of pace we went to Balboa Park. When we got there, we realized that it was December Nights, a festival full of food, drinks, shops, lights, and crowds of people. As Josh, I was not normally afraid of crowds, but as Molly, I was scared. I could have turned back, but with Crystal by my side I steeled myself to keep heading into the park. My fear evaporated as I was surrounded by hundreds of lights strung around the majestic park. It was magical! As Molly, I ate and drank and shopped, walking, for the first time, amongst the general public, rather than in "LGBT space." Though for most it would have been a simple night out, it taught me that Molly was not meant to be limited to certain (safe) areas. I realized that I felt free enough to be Molly outside of Hillcrest and Northpark, and I became confident enough to introduce Molly to my friends in Los Angeles, too. Though my boundaries had been vastly expanded, I still practiced caution, afraid of being caught or harassed.

My time with my ship and in San Diego was coming to an end and a new journey as an instructor at the Great Lakes Naval Training Command in Great Lakes, Illinois, awaited me. So, with a forlorn goodbye, we left our friends and Molly's birthplace to move to the Midwest. Before reaching our final destination, Crystal and I stopped in Tulsa, Oklahoma, to visit my mom and introduce my old high school buddies to Crystal. During this visit, I decided to come out to my mom as genderfluid and showed her pictures of Molly. She was startled and a little confused at first, but overall she was accepting. She never made me feel unwelcome or unloved. I know some trans people have gotten horrible reactions from their families, and I count myself lucky I was not one of them. Mom even remarked how much I looked like my cousin. Even though I was honest with my mom, I still kept Molly hidden from most of my friends except for one supportive buddy, Chris, who came out to me in high school. We remain very supportive of each other.

About a week later, I checked into my new command and started my instructor duty. The job itself was great. I loved sharing both my experience and knowledge with the newest crop of fire controlmen. Most of the people I worked with were cool; however, the area itself was awful. We were now living in the not-so-sprawling suburb of Round Lake, Illinois. Several sailors lived close to me and the only nearby places to go, like Gurnee Mills Mall, were overrun with Navy students and recent boot camp graduates. I had become used to letting Molly out a least once a week, but without a safe place to go I felt trapped. We finally found a movie theater forty-five minutes away. We made the drive at least once a month just so I could be myself. I had started to notice that if I went for any length of time without being Molly I would get cranky and moody. As we started making friends, we started exploring Chicago as Crystal and Molly. I would still avoid the major tourist attractions since sailors gravitated towards those. Instead, we spent our time in Ravenswood and few other Chicago neighborhoods with our friend "R." I would get dressed at their place to make the escape from suburbia easier. Having a local trans person really helped us make the most of a less than desirable duty station, especially since it was filled with some low points like my uncle and grandfather passing away and my mom moving to San Francisco. When I flew out for my grandfather's funeral, my friend Hayley had just had her bottom surgery, so mom and I swung by to visit Hayley and her mom. During our long conversations with Hayley, I discussed my gender fluidity, and remarked that I probably wouldn't seek hormones or surgery. At the time this was true, since I couldn't do either of those without tossing my career into the dumpster. What I didn't say was that I was insanely jealous of Hayley getting her outie turned into an innie, which should have been a tip-off that I might not have been as happy with my male self as I claimed to be. Despite my gender issues, I had a successful tour in Great Lakes and by the end of my tour I was the lead instructor for the schoolhouse. No one there knew about Molly, and I intended to keep my then-undiagnosed gender dysphoria a secret for the sake of my Navy career.

After teaching, I was to become the student. I was ordered to Dahlgren, Virginia, for AEGIS Weapon Supervisor (AWS) School. Dahlgren is a tiny town in the north of Virginia right on the Maryland border. I received temporary assigned duty (TAD) orders since I would be there less than six months. This meant that Crystal and I would be staying at the on-base Navy Lodge on the government's dime. This location was not conducive to letting Molly out at all. I threw myself into my motorcycling and video games to pass the time and keep my mind off things. I wore nighties to bed just so I could have that small bit of gender expression. I kept an even keel in school, keeping a high GPA even though inside I was going bonkers. Crystal did the best she could, using female pronouns when it felt safe. Luckily, Dan and Mel, some of my closest friends from San Diego, had also moved to Maryland and we visited them often. I came out to them as well, and although they were really supportive they suggested I not go out as Molly while visiting them. I think I would have been alright, but I followed their advice. I was happy enough to just be off base and we spent most of the time inside, gaming.

The huge thing that happened while I was in Dahlgren was that the ban on transgender service was finally dropped! I was super happy, even though I intended to continue serving as male. My decision was reinforced when, at a briefing, many students, all of whom were E-6s and E-7s, voiced their reluctance to serve next to an "icky trans sailor." I was heartbroken. I decided then to come out of my shell and try to educate them using the "genderbread" person (a gingerbread representation of gender expression, gender identity, and sexual orientation). I don't think I reached any of them. One person was worried that transgender people might join just to get surgery, but people join all the time to receive medical benefits, get an education, see the world, or just hit the reset button on their life! I reasoned that as long as someone serves honorably and gets the job done their reason for joining is a trivial matter. I still stand by that belief. Needless to say, I did not immediately come out.

After graduating in November of 2016, Crystal and I packed up to return to San Diego, from which my ship was slated to deploy a few weeks later. The day we got into San Diego, we toured an apartment, signed a lease, and checked into a hotel, and as soon as our bags were available I changed and Molly made her triumphant return to Hillcrest. Being back in what I consider my hometown and Molly's birthplace was so liberating! Crystal and I ate, drank, and visited old friends, which was great until I checked into my ship and discovered that I would be doing two deployments in the coming two years. The real kick to the gut was that our homeport would change to Pearl Harbor the following year. Here I had fought for the orders to San Diego only to be told we wouldn't be staying for very long and that most of that time I would be out to sea.

During the first deployment, I experienced a single, life-altering moment. I had just finished brushing my teeth and shaving when I looked in the mirror and found that the face staring back at me wasn't mine, it was Molly's. My mind's eye had erased my beard shadow, expertly applied my makeup, and lengthened my hair to match my wig. I was shocked, confused, and I couldn't look away. I had done my best to keep my life compartmentalized, but now Molly was nudging into my life where she didn't belong!

It is this moment I consider to be my epiphany. It was in that instant I realized I may have to change. I was terrified of going to my command and telling them I was trans and wanted to transition. These thoughts kept running through my mind. When we returned to San Diego, I told Crystal how I felt. We were both uneasy and concerned. When I had first discovered my gender fluidity, we had both attended the Trans Coming Out Group at the LGBT Center in Hillcrest. Now, after a three-year hiatus, we were happy to again be able to attend. In one particular meeting a junior enlisted sailor, Marcus, shared his story on how he had recently come out to his own command to positive support. That bolstered me to do the same. The next day I marched into medical and told them I was trans. It was both terrifying and liberating. It meant the world to me that our doc, a corpsman/medic, was very supportive. We made an appointment with mental health, which, unfortunately, was a few months out. I hated waiting, but there was not much I could do about it.

The very next day "the tweets" came out. My bowels turned to liquid. I was horrified. At this point I had put a decade into my career and did not want to toss that all away, but I couldn't stuff Molly back into a box either. Medical said I should keep my appointment even as Marcus's ship recommended he cancel his. Everybody was getting conflicting advice, but my mom had the best advice, which was to go see a therapist and keep it on the down low. I did so, paying out of my own pocket. Talking it out with the therapist helped immensely. I told her how I had doubts about my female gender identity since I had only discovered Molly later in life. I was never into girly things. I was always into Legos and Transformers, not Barbies or princesses. I never wanted to wear dresses or anything like that. Many of my trans friends and the stories I read always talked about how they enjoyed feminine toys and clothes when they were younger. With her help we worked through my qualms.

I realized that, yes, trans women can also be tomboyish. We covered how important and integral my military service was to me and how I couldn't imagine giving it up. We discussed how shaken I was from the president's tweets and how that threw my career into uncertainty. I told her everything. Talking with her was the best thing I could have done. Together we determined that, no matter what may come, Molly was here to stay. Crystal realized that she was probably going to end up with a wife instead of a husband, because, compared to my old self, she could see how happy I was as Molly.

By this time, I had informed my lower chain of command of what was going on. Without any official ban, I was able to talk with a military psychologist. I told her about seeing a civilian therapist, showed her pictures of Molly, and shared my experiences with her. I received my gender dysphoria diagnosis that day. With my diagnosis, the transgender care team drafted my gender transition plan, required of all service members who sought transition. The next step was to get the captain's approval. My captain was "old school" Navy, had risen from the enlisted ranks, and was the very picture of masculinity. It was a little intimidating to come up to his stateroom with my various senior people and inform him of my situation. We all sat down and he looked me in the eye and asked, "What's going on, Sackman?"

Stuffing down my hesitation, I replied, "Sir, I have been diagnosed with gender dysphoria and would like to transition under the Navy's guidance." I may be a little off on what I said, but I will never forget his response, "Oh is that all? I thought you were in trouble! Doc, we have procedures for this right?"

With the captain's blessing, I could continue my transition plan after deployment number two and, thankfully, this one was short, January to April. During this deployment, I also came out to a select portion of the crew, which basically means most of my ship as there are no secrets on a destroyer. No one said a word to me, but I knew they knew. Once we got back, I began my hormone regimen. I was ecstatic and hoped a few pills would instantly give me the body I wanted. Reality has been much slower, but progress was progress and a few months later I was excited to start developing breasts, albeit small ones. The time had come to tell the crew formally. The CO and I, plus my chain of command, the command master chief (senior enlisted leader), and a visiting chaplain squeezed into the captain's stateroom to discuss options. After a while, and lots of competing ideas, we hammered out a plan that had me being a guest speaker at a training on the topic. It took a few more months before we implemented this grand scheme. The end result is that I built a presentation they were happy with and was scheduled to deliver it all. My division officer said it might be a light showing since the ship's schedule was pretty full, but that went to hell when they called, "Muster the crew on the mess decks for transgender training." Sailors were piled deep and seating filled up fast. To top it off I had the Triad staring right at me: captain, executive officer, and command master chief, the top three people in charge of the ship. It took me a moment to find my voice. I was told later that it looked like I was about to crap myself. Despite the rough start, I got into it. I talked about the instruction and how it would affect others. At this point I hadn't come out. I was only teaching the policy. That changed when I got into executing the process. Standing in front of my entire ship, I said, "The reason I am giving this training is that I am transgender and here are the steps I am taking." I told my shipmates everything I had done to get to that point, including sharing my gender treatment plan. I had a few sailors congratulate me afterwards. It felt good to be honest with my ship, because as my CO likes to say, we are a family. It may be a cliché statement, but it's true. On a warship you live, sleep, and eat with everyone. There is very little privacy and we rely on each other for survival, whether in peace or at war.

I have since completed my treatment plan and the Navy now recognizes me as my true gender. I no longer live in two worlds of pretending to be male at work and being my female self at home. I've moved into female berthing (living space on board ship) and wear female uniforms now. My transition is complete according to the military. To me it's not. I wear a wig to cover my still growing hair. I have had an orchiectomy (testicle removal) but can't get full bottom surgery until I rotate off the ship in 2022. People still slip up and use male pronouns, but these are minor complaints. I've also had people leave encouraging notes on my bed in berthing. My wife has stuck with me, reveling with me after each small victory in my transition. I can't ask for much more. I am fortunate that my struggles have been relatively small; I know there are trans siblings of mine who are suffering in the military and the civilian world just to be themselves. I hope they can find the strength to continue—the sacrifices are worth it all. I know my decision to transition has been the right one. To anyone that is trans that might be reading this, just know that you can do this and you are loved.

Miranda Jones, Lieutenant Colonel, U.S. Marine Corps, 1989–2019

I served in the Marine Corps for thirty years. For my first twenty years of service, I was an infantryman, both enlisted and officer. For the last ten years, I have served as an acquisitions officer, which means I managed various aspects of defense systems through development, production, procurement, and disposal. Today I teach these skills to others in defense systems acquisition. With an infantry background, that meant that most of my assignments were kinetic-weapons based—that is, rifles and such. I have deployed many times in my career, three times in combat. In all of my time, I felt surrounded by the hypermasculinity of warriors whose purpose was to wreak havoc on an enemy, whichever enemy they were pointed toward. I immersed myself in that culture, dressing myself in all of its trappings, both internal and external. That is what Marines do. We train to be the deadliest killers we can be and stand by, waiting for the order to unleash all of our fury. Throughout my three decades of wearing the uniform, I lived in that mindset. That mindset helped me cover up and avoid the person who was always inside of me like an annoying debtor asking for their due. I chose to ignore her in the hope that she would go away. If I detected her presence, I would shake her off like a pitcher on the mound who does not like the catcher's call. If she crept into my conversation or expression, I would run from her, pretending she was never there and, more importantly, hoping no one noticed. As long as no one else noticed, I could "not notice" her either and go back to burying that transgender part of me.

What does being transgender mean to me? It means my gender crosses society's common boundaries of strictly male or female. It does not mean I am confused. I know for sure that I am not 100 percent male or 100 percent female inside and that my comfort zone shifts without warning. "Being transgender" does not ask me if it is a good time to comment on something pretty or have a compassionate emotion toward someone's plight. This is something that has always been hard for me to keep to myself, not blurting it out in public for everyone to hear. What does that mean for my military service? It means that I have had to make sure not to let on that I had feelings that went against the ethos, an ethos which had been drilled into my head from the moment I stepped on to those fabled yellow footprints. It meant that I had to develop a defense mechanism within me, enabling me to brush aside my gentler, more compassionate traits to the point of denying and even attacking their characteristics.

In order to blend in effectively, one must take on the appearance of one's surroundings. We call it camouflage. I was a master of camouflage in this manly man's world, joining in and even leading the verbal charge against all things "girly" and "weak." These things did not belong in our world of killing machines. We were the epitome of manly men and, as Marines, we were expected to be those manly men as a matter of course. We had to make it look natural. That level of killer instinct could not be developed. It must be something with which we were born. It had to be in in our very DNA. At least that was the story we told ourselves and anyone else who would listen. We pushed that story like a political campaign, harder and louder. We had to. To admit that any of us may not be everything that our caricatured existence had been built up to be was to show weakness. We were Marines. We did not have weaknesses . . . at least not that we showed anyone . . . and least of all ourselves.

I enjoy being able to express myself as a woman. I enjoy the feminine mannerisms that I am able to display when I dress and that, for me in my military life, are off-limits otherwise. I feel very much as though I am expressing a part of myself that is and always has been inside me. This is not just a hobby that is fun for a fleeting moment, and I most certainly do not feel guilty about it! It feels right, even perfect. There was no struggle for me when I was growing up, as I never focused on, nor was I confused by, these feminine feelings. I did not let them confuse me. I just shrugged them off, as if to say, "Boys don't do that sort of thing," and off I went down my path wearing my custom-fit blinders. I feel a bit like a dimwit now for not recognizing what I was doing, but it was not a problem for me when I was growing up.

This has all been a relatively recent discovery for me, about two years now, but not one around which I am at all unsure. I did not grow up feeling that something was wrong or different about myself. However, upon reflection, my discovery and self-revelation has made some parts of my younger years make a little more sense. As you can imagine, I have not taken this lightly and have spent more energy reflecting, learning, and even getting counseling in order to better understand and learn to manage this within my life.

There is a feminine component to my personality and who I am at my deepest core. This is an obvious contrast to who I am on the outside most of the time. Most of the time, I am as stereotypically male as the next husband, father, athlete, hunter, shooting sports enthusiast, car mechanic, or infantry combat veteran. I am all of these things all of the time. Under it all, I am also Miranda, all of the time. I consider myself to be transgender—bi-gender to be more specific—to attach a label, if you feel you need one. I use that term as an umbrella for all people who have any incongruence between their outward body and inward soul with respect to gender. I do not have any desire to physically transition or to live as a woman full-time. But I am still transgender.

The lifting of the ban on transgendered military service allowed an unconscious switch to flip in my brain, opening my ability to hear and a willingness for me to face the questions that I had suppressed throughout my whole life. I have likened the experiences of my life to a sort of intellectual laziness where I would ignore and brush off the feelings of femininity that might enter my mind from time to time. As noted above, it was easier to deal with them as "boys don't think that way" or "boys don't behave that way," and I would cram those emotions and traits deep down inside. I crammed them so far down inside me, in fact, that I did not feel them at all. I did not realize I had done this and did not notice them there. I did not allow myself to look.

There was no dysphoria for me. There was no inclination of longing to be a woman or to even just be able to express those female characteristics that are definitely part of my whole and that I can now recognize, embrace, and express publicly, albeit with some level of caution and guarded openness. In lifting the ban, the Department of Defense told the world it is all right to be that person and that one can be honest with oneself and each other about your gender. My identity did not conform to the strict binary that had been shellacked with layer upon layer of varnish over my entire military career thus far. A window of opportunity had been opened for me to look into and eventually out of. I had always turned away from that window, denying its very existence.

Had I been able to face my own gender in its entirety, I would have been far more effective in demonstrating the compassion necessary to lead and support my Marines dealing with the aftereffects of combat. I would have been more adept and comfortable telling them that their experiences today, because of their experiences on the battlefield, were okay. I would have been better at reassuring them that each of us is unique and that we each experience a spectrum of emotions. Most important, I would have been able to assure them that their unique journey is no less valid than any other. The heavily overdosed machismo that we had all been bombarded with throughout our time in uniform overwrote any of that and perpetuated the myth that it was definitely not okay to feel emotions that were anything less than hypermasculine.

There's an old cartoon with a Marine inside a glass case equipped for battle. Inside the glass case, a caption says, "Break glass in case of war." The implication was that we could not be integrated with society because we were so especially off-the-charts barbaric and utterly uncontrollable in our quest to annihilate anything in our way that we must be held in special reserve only for the most violent of purposes. Of course, perpetuating this ideal in our daily operating and training was accomplished by daily brainwashing to the same effect. Any sign of weakness was pounced upon and ripped apart. Any expression of sensitivity or appreciation for beauty was always met with deriding comments as to "her" unmanliness. "Don't be a bitch" or "Nice work, Sally" were common verbal weapons used when someone came up even remotely short in any physical endeavor. It was like some of the early scenes in the book *Ender's Game* in which Ender is derided for being weak, too weak for military service. As the story develops, though, we discover that perhaps physical attributes are not all that are required to make a good and effective leader. Too bad this part of the book was never discussed in any of the professional military education sessions I experienced. We certainly didn't talk about how diversity might be a good thing or even a force multiplier. The environment cultivated and even rewarded by the exclusionary mindset of homogeneous and one-size-fits-all personality expectations would not allow such open-mindedness. This has been my military experience as a transgender Marine.

My story is not as direct as others may be. I did not face discharge from service based on my gender identity. Might I have, if I had found the strength to explore my own feelings earlier? Perhaps. That is sort of the point, though, too. Because there was no room in my super-grunt world for that sort of introspection and openness, I was never able to discover some of the most compassionate and valuable traits of my whole self. I was not able to demonstrate the best understanding possible of my troops' experiences and communicate the empathy for them that they deserved. That was left up to the behavioral health counselors, but only if one was "weakened" enough to the point they were even willing to admit they needed help. I survived a testosterone poisoning of another kind. It is as if I was wearing a testosterone patch, supplemented occasionally by a painful injection of "Man up" when I neither wanted or needed it, and which more often than not painfully missed the vein like a drunk nurse and may have done more harm than good in the end.

Natalie Seidel, Petty Officer Second Class, U.S. Navy, 2012–Present

Having entered the service in 2012 after teaching junior high and high school before becoming a Navy man, I was a late bloomer. I loved working with those kids. I was absolutely terrified on my first day teaching, but once that first day was done I was so happy. Teaching was great. One of the experiences I took away from the experience was seeing these kids going through puberty. At this point in my life, it was difficult at best for me to even consider the possibility that I had been anything but a man. It was outside the realm of possibility for me to even consider transitioning. I had known that since I was thirteen myself that I was different, knowing that I had wished and even prayed that I woke up as a girl the next day. But, for me, being an observer to their experience was a good jumping-off point for understanding my own second puberty. On the one hand, I had some idea of what I might go through because I'd been through the ravages of hormones, but with puberty 2.0, it's doing all sorts of different things to me that I've never experienced. At least through this one, if I really want to, I can legally go to the bar at the end of the day.

In 2010, I was laid off and went from being a full-time teacher working in Hawaii to moving back in with my parents, spending two years substitute teaching and applying to about three hundred different schools during that time. I was aimless for a while, eventually realizing that I needed to make a lateral move of some sort, but really getting out of my comfort zone.

My father was a linguist with the Air Force, and that had always been something that interested me and touched on my academic side. Figuring I'd build on that heritage, I joined the Navy, leaving for boot camp as a twenty-seven-year-old man.

Fast-forward a bit. I went through my training, met a wonderful woman who became my wife, and was stationed in Georgia. In 2015, there I was, deep in the Bible Belt, when I finally had a realization that I'm a woman. After all these years, I'd connected the dots. I didn't know how to approach it, but it is who I am. I came out to my wife, and initially we had some problems, but she spoke with some family of hers and her best friends from back home. She realized that she loved me for the person I am, not as a gendered person. We're still together and about to celebrate our five-year anniversary.

In 2016, when Secretary of Defense Ashton Carter released guidance allowing transgender people to serve openly, I began to be a bit more open with some of our close friends. Being in Georgia, I never felt comfortable coming out publicly. I started doing research and figured out everything transition-related from start to finish. But I was biding my time because I knew that as much as I wanted to start this journey, I didn't feel safe doing that in Georgia.

In 2017, I deployed to the Middle East and was there for six months, where I had to be completely closeted. Somehow, I kept myself strong. I journaled, writing down everything I could to reaffirm myself. That year was tough, especially with the July tweets. I was devastated.

I didn't know what was going to happen at that point or if I'd ever be able to serve openly. I thought, "Well, it's never going to happen now." However, by sheer luck, I received orders transferring me to Maryland. That was easily one of the best things that could have happened to me, to us.

In January 2018, with our two dogs, my wife and I moved to Maryland with a blizzard behind our tracks. We still had a dozen boxes or so piled up all over the house, but I had to start work. I saw a lot of familiar faces. One of them, someone who had been an ally of mine since day one and on the hunch that I was transgender, asked me if I wanted to meet somebody. That somebody turned out to be Petty Officer First Class Alice Ashton, another trans woman. She's been a big advocate for the trans community and has single-handedly guided me through the process for everything from applying for my military treatment plan to helping me with my gender marker change, which I'm now within weeks of completing. I will be forever thankful to my friend for introducing me because I don't know where I would be otherwise. I'm now a member of SPARTA and I've met many other supportive people in that group.

I received a diagnosis of gender dysphoria in April of 2018. At that point, given the uncertainty in the wake of the president's tweets, people were afraid of what was going to happen. We still are, but it doesn't prevent us from living. I decided that it was way more important for me to live, and live healthily, than to continue living the lie that I'd been telling myself: that I was okay. I developed the philosophy that while some people view my dysphoria diagnosis as a scarlet letter, I view it as a badge of courage.

That courage allowed me to finally take the steps I need for the self-care that I had denied myself for so many years. I started hormones in September 2018 and have a care plan to address additional medical requirements. I've legally changed my name and am waiting for Navy administration to catch up. My commanding officer signed off on everything and has been nothing but a staunch supporter.

The disheartening part, and an absolute pain, is that I've had to live by the male standards for everything, from not being able to grow my hair out to not being allowed to wear makeup at work or use the restrooms in which I belong. The burden of getting my gender marker changed and of not receiving an exception to policy (ETP) has been tremendous. My commanding officer (CO) didn't even submit my current ETP request until February 2019. He kept getting different legal advice from people and then his immediate superior changed. With all that, I had to submit three different versions of the ETP within six months. My CO told me that he's tired of this because there's no reason why this shouldn't have been approved already.

Right now, I feel as if I'm fighting a war on two fronts. On one side, there is a literal threat, in the form of the current policy, to our livelihoods and our means to provide for ourselves and our families. All we want to do is to be able to serve, for whatever reason we serve. For a lot of us, being transgender is far from the most interesting thing about us. There are so many more facets to our lives. On the other side, there's a fight being waged with public perception. We just want to be seen as people. We're not sex-deranged perverts or mentally confused. We are just people on this great blue ball called earth who want to be able to live their best life possible. Instead of burying something that has killed many of us over the years, we are taking risks every day to be openly public or to just live as ourselves, fearing violence for being ourselves.

Going forward, we need to continue to show that not only can we do these difficult military jobs, but that we do these jobs well and to the point where nobody questions our ability. It should not be a matter of "Is this person trans or not?" or "What is this person carrying in their pants?" Instead it should be "What is this person capable of doing for the country?"

I view the trans ban as a blip in our history. I have faith in the American people in that we will find a positive resolution. Americans also expect a fair deal, especially for those of us who wear the cloth of our nation. Service members give up time with our friends, families, and loved ones. Some of us never come back from our service, whether that's in the literal sense or psychologically. But we too expect a fair deal. I see the tide changing for the better, especially for the trans community and in spite of everything that's happening. I present masculine at work but can still be Natalie, and standards of medical care are rapidly improving. I have to believe that we'll look back on this episode and do our best to not repeat it with another group of people.

PART III

Going Forward

6

Serving in the Future

I've been told three times that something other than my capability to do the job was the reason I wasn't worthy of an opportunity. First for my gender assigned at birth, second for my sexual orientation prior to transition, and third for my gender identity.

—Lieutenant Commander Blake Dremann

On April 12, 2019, the ban on transgender service came into effect. Anyone who hadn't received a diagnosis of gender dysphoria from a military doctor prior to that date would no longer be allowed to receive transition related medical care, even if deemed necessary by their doctor. No new transgender recruits would be allowed into the service unless they agreed to serve in their sex assigned at birth. The approximately sixteen hundred service members who came out in the brief window where they could have done so were exempt from this policy, but they were now an endangered species as no one else would be joining their ranks.

Among those who would be denied entry under the new policy was Map Pesqueira, a first-year student and trans man at the University of Texas at Austin, who would lose his Reserve Officers' Training Corps scholarship. SPARTA president Blake Dremann said, at the time, "Map Pesqueira is the first, but sadly won't be the last. Map is qualified, capable, and willing to serve. The only reason he can't is a discriminatory policy that costs this nation our future heroes."[1] Indeed, while Pesqueira's story grabbed the headlines, he is not alone. We will never know how many people, ready, able, and wishing to serve in the nation's military, have been denied that opportunity.

In March 2019, Adam Smith (D-WA), chair of the House Armed Services Committee, stated that the ban was "an insult to transgender individuals who have served and are still serving with distinction," adding that "[a]nyone who is qualified and willing should be allowed to serve their country openly."[2] Whether it is the general public, military personnel across the ranks, the Joint Chiefs, or within the U.S. Congress, widespread support for trans military service is apparent. Yet an unknown number of trans people had remained in limbo about their futures. A number of these individuals were not yet serving but wished to do so. We turn now to a few such stories.

As a sixteen-year-old high school student who was severely bullied for being "different," Jody "saw the military as a way of both finding a way to pay for college and an attempt at 'manning up.'" She describes "once and for all putting away all of these thoughts and feelings that I was really a girl, not the man that everyone thought I was."[3] Jody served as an armor crewman and cavalry scout in the Ohio Army National Guard from 1987 to 1995 and hopes to serve again. Her story is somewhat reminiscent of that of Joanna Clark, who had served admirably, left the service, and returned only to be discharged nineteen months later. Jody writes:

> I'm working as a nurse and social worker, dedicated to helping the LGBTQIA population of central Ohio. In 2017, a few weeks before Trump's tweets, I talked to a recruiter and started trying to meet the standards to rejoin the Ohio Army National Guard, this time as an officer and social worker. It was not easy for me, having gained close to 30 pounds after bottom surgery in 2016. But I was determined to do all I could to join. Over the course of ten months, I lost 50 pounds. Leading up to start of ban that went into effect in 2019, I'd met all the requirements to get in, and received a waiver for a history of anxiety. I was so close![4]

Jody then had to pause her efforts when an X-ray revealed an area of concern on her back. She had given up when she heard about a local man who had returned from service, had trouble adjusting, and committed suicide. She writes, "I shook the hands of the grieving parents. I felt helpless. It felt like an avoidable tragedy, so many damaged lives. I am a social worker, and I want to help soldiers transition back into civilian life. I knew that night that I had to try again . . . ."[5]

As of this writing, having resolved her back issue, Jody awaits a decision as to whether or not she has been selected to serve as a captain with a combat stress unit in the U.S. Army Reserve. Jody writes, "I don't want to look at another dead soldier without knowing that I did everything in my power to be in a position of service to this great country, once more."[6]

Others have never served but wish to do so. Marcus knew from a very young age that he wanted to serve his country. He says, "I knew it would be a hard life but a life with purpose, and an accomplishment I could be proud of when I was older."[7] Having experienced several bumps in the road as a student and while transitioning, when the repeal of the ban was announced in 2016, Marcus decided to enlist. He hired a tutor and spent the entire summer of 2017 studying for the military entrance exam. He did well and decided to pursue admission to the Coast Guard. While the first recruiter was helpful, he would soon be retiring. Marcus writes:

> I had to start over with a brand new recruiter with no experience. Between June and November of 2018 this recruiter gave me the run around, ignoring my phone calls, emails, and text messages. I called him once a day for over a month before he would set up a meeting and give me lukewarm answers to my questions. Meetings with him felt like I was in a Groundhog Day Twilight Zone. All information went in one ear and out the other, he was just reading from a script and going through the motions. He never remembered any details from previous meetings or phone discussions and would make copies of the same documents he already made copies of a few weeks earlier. I knew he was playing games, but there was nothing I could do.[8]

Despite his efforts, Marcus writes that "by the end of March [the recruiter] called and told me that the new policy would prohibit my use of testosterone and keep me from serving. I was furious. My patience with this recruiter was on empty and I knew my time had run out. . . . I was heartbroken and defeated. . . . However, I am stubborn, and I am extremely persistent. I don't intend to give up until I get that final rejection letter from Washington for me to frame on the wall."[9]

Among those wishing to join the military, a select few were publicly fighting to do so. Earlier, we mentioned the four cases that were working their way through the courts. Ryan Karnoski is one of the plaintiffs challenging the ban. In recalling his early interest in military service, Ryan writes:

> I remember the passing of my cousin, Michael, a helicopter pilot with the Army's venerable 160th Special Operations Aviation Regiment (SOAR), the Night Stalkers. I struggled to make sense of the grief that emanated from the loss of a family member. However, the process of reconciling this grief forced me to reflect on the true extent of the sacrifices that service members make to honor their commitment to the tasks set forth for them by the leaders of our country. I felt compelled to join the military to work directly with others who had made this commitment to our country.[10]

Instead of joining at that time, Ryan pursued his education. Having completed his undergraduate degree and while pursuing a master's in social work (MSW), he again began thinking about military service. He learned about the military's Social Work Internship Program and contacted a recruiter to learn more. Shortly after graduating with his MSW, he woke up to the tweets that, as he describes it, "would put an indefinite pause on my goal to join the military as a social worker."[11] Still wishing to serve, Ryan decided to challenge the ban.

We would be remiss if we didn't also acknowledge those who entered military service prior to the April 2019 ban going into effect, but who were unable to complete the tasks necessary to be protected by the "grandfather" clause. Some were simply not ready, others had not yet realized they were trans. Valerie, a trans woman who, under the 2019 policy, had to continue presenting as male, illustrates the heartache for this group of service members. She writes:

> I am a transgender airman[12] working in cyber systems operations under the Air Force Global Strike Command. Our mission is to support and conduct nuclear deterrence and global strike operations, and I am proud to be serving my country and protecting the freedom of all Americans. Nothing comes before my commitment to serve . . . .[13]

Under the policy crafted by the Trump administration, Valerie's only hope was to be granted a waiver allowing her to serve as an openly transgender person. She writes, "It has been a stressful and uphill battle. Each day requires that I present a fake version of myself. Being able to serve openly and to be myself would mean everything to me, relieving the constant weight and struggle of putting my feelings in a box and living a lie."[14]

We know that there appears to be support for the open service of trans service members. The week following President Trump's tweets, a Morning Consult/POLITICO poll revealed that in response to the question "Do you believe the U.S. military should allow current transgender members of the U.S. military to continue serving?" 68 percent of 1,972 registered voters said yes. To the question "Do you believe the U.S. military should allow transgender individuals to newly join the military?" 55 percent of 1,972 registered voters said yes.[15] Almost two years later, in May 2019, a Gallup poll asked the question "Do you favor or oppose allowing openly transgender men and women to serve in the military?" Seventy-one percent responded that they favored doing so.[16]

In research conducted between August 2017 and March 2018, Dunlap et al. analyzed data gathered from 486 heterosexual cisgender and lesbian, gay, and bisexual cisgender active duty military individuals with regard to their support for transgender military personnel. Their findings "indicate broad support for transgender military service across all four branches of the military and military ranks."[17] Sixty-six percent of those surveyed supported transgender service. Though the greatest levels of support were found among lesbian, gay, and bisexual and cisgender women service members, all groups had support levels that exceeded 55 percent.

In 2018, almost two years after transgender service members began open service, the service chiefs of the Army, Navy, and Air Force, the commandant of the Marine Corps, and the incoming commandant of the Coast Guard testified before Congress that a policy of trans inclusion had not undermined cohesion, one of the concerns most often cited as a basis for exclusionary policies. For example, Army Chief of Staff Mark Milley stated, "I have received precisely zero reports of issues of cohesion, discipline, morale and all those sorts of things."[18]

While difficult to quantify, especially when some remain invisible, when we consider the myriad contributions made by trans service members, a tiny fraction of which are documented here, it seems difficult not to accept that their presence benefits the military. Less challenging is showing how a ban on their service harms the military. In November 2020, the Palm Center released a report in which it found that "the overall impact of the ban has been to harm readiness by compromising recruitment, reputation, retention, unit cohesion, morale, medical care, and good order and discipline."[19]

On February 29, 2020, presidential candidate Joe Biden stated, "[O]n day one of my presidency, I will begin reinstating LGBTQ protections President Trump has rolled back, including ensuring transgender individuals can openly serve in the military."[20] In a memo dated December 28, 2020, the Palm Center noted that, under a new administration, "the ban can be reversed in under thirty days through executive action."[21] Doing so does not require Congressional action. On January 25, 2021, President Biden signed an executive order stating, in part, that "it shall be the policy of the United States to ensure that all transgender individuals who wish to serve in the United States military and can meet the appropriate standards shall be able to do so openly and free from discrimination."[22] This executive order revokes the memos of the previous administration barring the military service of transgender personnel. The executive order also reads, "It is my conviction as Commander in Chief of the Armed Forces that gender identity should not be a bar to military service."[23]

On March 31, 2021, President Biden announced the new policy allowing transgender individuals to serve openly. The policy went into effect on April 30, 2021. While full implementation may take time, thousands of transgender service members waiting for their opportunity to reach their full potential are bursting with excitement. Many others are looking to the future and how we make the policies of open transgender service better and enable a more diverse and inclusive military ready to meet the challenges of the 21st century.

Despite the optimism, there is still concern. Will the administration that follows Biden again attempt to turn back the clock? As Lieutenant Colonel Bree Fram said in an interview with NPR's Ailsa Chang, "We need legislative action to prevent a future administration from flipping the switch, and we'll speak with legislators at any opportunity we can about the value of the opportunity for service."[24] If Congress fails to do so, and individuals like those whose stories you see here continue to serve, will the prospect of a military without transgender people be just as unconscionable as it is to think of today's military without African Americans, women, or lesbians, gays, and bisexuals? We'd like to think so.

ACKNOWLEDGMENTS

We could not have produced this book without the dedication, commitment, and contributions of a wide range of individuals. First and foremost is everyone who expressed an interest in the project, from those who agreed to share the call for participants to those willing to write or be interviewed. While we were not able to write with, speak with, or quote everyone, we remain incredibly grateful for their interest and support. Of course, the volume you hold in your hands would not exist were it not for the contributors, both writers and interviewees, who offered us their time, energy, and trust. If we said "thank you" a thousand times, another would be warranted. Finally, we thank every trans member of the military—past, present, and future—for serving, despite the challenges, as well as the allies who support/ed them.

I, Máel Embser-Herbert, would like to thank Joe Ippolito, founder and executive director of the Gender Reel film festival, and Tarrence Robertson-Bayless (MAJ, Ret.), Minnesota Army National Guard, for providing the inspiration to further explore the transgender military experience. Gratitude is also due to my friend and fellow veteran Josh Gershick, whose book *Secret Service* provided me with a model for how I might best share the experiences of trans service members. Boundless appreciation goes to my friend Ann Verme, whose editorial eagle eye was invaluable. MJ Luna, who provided research and drafting for the introduction, Ally Gall, and Najma Omar were incredibly helpful—and it's always great to have students along for the ride. Thanks, of course, to my departmental colleagues, Valerie Chepp, Susi Keefe, Ryan LeCount, and Sharon Preves, who can always be counted on for unending good cheer, and to Marcela Kostihová and Robin Parritz for their continued support and enthusiasm. I was truly thankful when Bree Fram agreed to join me on this journey. Having been away from military service for twenty years, her insight, contributions, and networks were critical. This is the part where you know you're going to forget someone. Having begun scholarship on gender, sexuality, and the military over three decades ago, there's such a long list of those who have played a key role in my work. Please know that I am thankful for your support, despite a lengthy list of names not appearing here. Jennifer Hammer, Ilene Kalish, Sonia Tsuruoka, and their colleagues at New York University Press, as well as our anonymous reviewers, also deserve my thanks. I am so glad to again have had the opportunity to work with NYU. I will continue to sing your praises.

I, Bree Fram, would like to thank my family and particularly my wife, Peg Fram, for sticking by my side on this crazy journey of ours. In addition to the often-overlooked hardships of being a military spouse, she's faced a more difficult path than my own simply for loving me and has enabled me to reach for the stars. I'm grateful to Máel Embser-Herbert for reaching out to invite me to be a co-editor. They are an outstanding scholar and a pleasure to work with. Thank you to the amazing team at SPARTA that has done so much to advance the cause of transgender service, to Blake Dremann for his leadership, and for all the transgender service members that lace up their boots and complete the mission of the U.S. military every day even in the face of hardship. I'd like to thank the first transgender friends I made in Denver, who connected me through a chain of friends on to SPARTA in 2014 when I was just beginning to understand myself. It's hard to imagine finding my courage without any of you. I'm forever in debt to all my amazing friends, colleagues, and superiors who have given me nothing but love and support over the years. Finally, I want to thank my kids, Kathryn and Alivya, for making me the proudest Maddy on the planet.

NOTES

Preface

1. "GLAAD Media Reference Guide—Transgender," GLAAD, accessed August 4, 2020, www.glaad.org.
2. Jeremy Lybarger, "Lou Sullivan's Diaries Are a Radical Testament to Trans Happiness," *New Yorker*, September 16, 2019, www.newyorker.com.
3. Malaysia Walker, "ACLU Mississippi, Highlight: Lucy Hicks Anderson, a Black Trans Pioneer," ACLU Mississippi, accessed August 4, 2020, www.aclu-ms.org.
4. "Digital Transgender Archive: Global Terms," accessed August 4, 2020, www. digitaltransgenderarchive.net.

Introduction

1. Know Your Military, U.S. Department of Defense, accessed February 29, 2020, www.defense.gov.
2. Gary J. Gates and Jody L. Herman, "Transgender Military Service in the United States," Williams Institute, May 2014, https://williamsinstitute.law.ucla.edu.
3. Rupert Neville, "Adventurous Lives of Women in Trousers," clipping, 1910, Digital Transgender Archive, accessed February 29, 2020, www.digitaltransgenderarchive. net.
4. "The Chevalier d'Éon," National Portrait Gallery, accessed December 20, 2020, www.npg.org.uk.
5. "William Brown, 'a female African,'" National Archives, Black Presence: Asian and Black History in Britain 1500–1850, accessed February 29, 2020, www.nationalar-chives.gov.uk.
6. Ibid.
7. "Albert Cashier aka Jennie Hodgers," American Battlefield Trust, accessed February 29, 2020, www.battlefields.org.
8. Deanne Blanton and Lauren M. Cook, *They Fought Like Demons: Women Soldiers in the Civil War* (New York: Vintage Books, 2002), 173.
9. "Females Posed as Men," clipping, 1901, Digital Transgender Archive, accessed February 29, 2020, www.digitaltransgenderarchive.net.
10. Ibid.
11. Blanton and Cook, *They Fought Like Demons*, 208.
12. "TS Discharged from Naval Reserve," *Drag* 7, no. 26, 6.
13. Ibid.

14. Ibid, 7.
15. Sister Mary Elizabeth Clark, Wikipedia, accessed February 29, 2020, https://en.wikipedia.org.
16. Sharon Ann Stuart, "Military Law Project: Sharon Stuart, Atty.," speech, 1992, Digital Transgender Archive, accessed February 29, 2020, www.digitaltransgenderarchive.net.
17. Sharon Ann Stuart, "Report from the Military Project," speech, 1993, Digital Transgender Archive, accessed February 29, 2020, www.digitaltransgenderarchive.net.
18. Ibid.
19. Sharon Ann Stuart, "Report from the Rights Project: Military Law, the Bill of Gender Rights, the Imprisonment Watch and Family Law," speech, 1994, Digital Transgender Archive, accessed February 29, 2020, www.digitaltransgenderarchive.net. For additional commentary on the questionnaire and data collection, see Lynn Hubschman, *Transsexuals: Life from Both Sides* (Darby, PA: Diane Publishing Company, 2000), 209–210.
20. Research and drafting of text by Hamline University student MJ Luna served as a foundation for the development of the material that appears in this section.
21. We use the term "homosexual" when quoting or referring to more medicalized frameworks in which same-sex sexuality is being addressed. To make the prose less cumbersome, we have also chosen to use "gay" as shorthand for lesbian, gay, and bisexual, particularly when referencing a time in which that was the common parlance.
22. Defense Force Management, "DOD's Policy on Homosexuality," United States General Accounting Office, June 1992, 2, http://archive.gao.gov.
23. Melissa Sheridan Embser-Herbert, *The U.S. Military's "Don't Ask, Don't Tell" Policy: A Reference Handbook* (Westport, CT: Praeger Security International, 2002), 9.
24. Nathaniel Frank, *Unfriendly Fire: How the Gay Ban Undermines the Military and Weakens America* (New York: Thomas Dunne Books, 2002), 86.
25. Ibid., 65.
26. "Policy Implications of Lifting the Ban on Homosexuals in the Military, Hearings before the Committee on Armed Services," House of Representatives, May 4 and 5, 1993, U.S. Government Printing Office: Washington, DC, 290.
27. Embser-Herbert, *The U.S. Military's "Don't Ask, Don't Tell" Policy*, 12.
28. Frank, *Unfriendly Fire*, 215.
29. Candace West and Don H. Zimmerman, "Doing Gender," *Gender & Society* 1, no. 2 (June 1987): 125–151, www.jstor.org. The published article was based in part on a paper presented at the Annual Meeting of the American Sociological Association in September 1977.
30. See, for example, Melissa S. Herbert, *Camouflage Isn't Only for Combat: Gender, Sexuality, and Women in the Military* (New York: New York University Press,

1998), and Dawne Moon, Theresa W. Tobin, and J. E. Sumerau, "Alpha, Omega, and the Letters in Between: LGBTQI Conservative Christians Undoing Gender," *Gender & Society* 33, no. 4 (August 2019): 583–606, https://doi. org/10.1177/0891243219846592.

31. West and Zimmerman, "Doing Gender," 125.
32. In 1997, *Gender & Society* published Patricia Gagne, Richard Tewksbury, and Deanna McGaughey's article, "Coming Out and Crossing Over: Identity Formation and Proclamation in a Transgender Community," centered on interviews with sixty-five "masculine-to-feminine transgenderists [*sic*]" and their coming out experiences.
33. In three recent *Gender & Society* articles, Catherine Connell ("Doing, Undoing, or Redoing Gender?: Learning from the Workplace Experiences of Transpeople") also uses the "doing gender" framework to explore the experiences of trans people in the workplace; Garrison, in their work on trans identity ("On the Limits of 'Trans Enough': Authenticating Trans Identity Narratives"), addresses gender as an interactional accomplishment; and, relevant to any consideration of the military, Nik M. Lampe, Shannon K. Carter, and J. E. Sumerau "examine the ways gendered frames shift to make room for societal changes while maintaining existing pillars of systemic gender inequality" ("Continuity and Change in Gender Frames: The Case of Transgender Reproduction").
34. Andrew Grissom, *Transgender Individuals and Military Service Bibliography*, American Library Association, accessed February 28, 2020, www.ala.org.
35. James E. Parco, David A. Levy, and Sarah R. Spears, "Beyond DADT Repeal: Transgender Evolution within the U.S. Military," *International Journal of Transgenderism* 17, no. 1 (2016): 4–13, https://doi.org/10.1080/15532739.2015.109566 9.
36. Máel Embser-Herbert, "'Welcome! Oh, Wait . . .': Transgender Military Service in a Time of Uncertainty," *Sociological Inquiry* 90, no. 2 (May 2020): 405–429, https://doi.org/10.1111/soin.12329.

Chapter 1. The Battle for Open Service

1. Bree Fram, personal communication, November 11, 2019.
2. Chris Geidner, "Military Group Picks Trans Woman as Leader," BuzzFeed News, October 25, 2012, www.buzzfeednews.com.
3. Sunnivie Brydum, "Transgender Group Leaves OutServe-SLDN, Joins Startup Group SPART*A," *Advocate*, July 22, 2013, www.advocate.com.
4. Chuck Hadad, Susan Chun, and Dana Ford, "Transgender Ex-Navy SEAL Lives in 'Gray World.'" CNN.com, September 4, 2014, www.cnn.com.
5. Joycelyn Elders and Alan M. Steinman, *Report of the Transgender Military Service Commission*. Palm Center, March 2014, www.palmcenter.org.
6. Helen Nakashima, "Hagel: Policies on Transgender Personnel Serving in the Military Should Be Reviewed," *Washington Post*, May 11, 2014, www.washingtonpost.com.

7. "Defense Secretary Ashton Carter Addresses Transgender Service," Human Rights Campaign, Press Releases, February 22, 2015, accessed February 29, 2020, www.hrc.org.
8. Bree Fram, personal communication, December 25, 2019.
9. Bree Fram, personal communication, January 2, 2020.
10. Secretary of the Air Force Public Affairs, "Air Force Elevates Discharge Authority for Transgender-Related Airmen Separations," June 4, 2015, accessed February 29, 2020, www.af.mil.
11. Bree Fram, personal communication, October 27, 2019.
12. "Statement by Secretary of Defense Ash Carter on DOD Transgender Policy," July 13, 2015, accessed February 29, 2020, www.defense.gov.
13. Bree Fram, personal communication, October 27, 2019.
14. Terri Moon Cronk, "Transgender Service Members Can Now Serve Openly, Carter Announces," June 30, 2016, accessed February 29, 2020, www.defense.gov.
15. Donald J. Trump (@realDonaldTrump), "Thank you to the LGBT community!" Twitter, June 14, 2016, https://twitter.com/realDonaldTrump/status/742771576039460864.
16. Trump Accountability Project, GLAAD, accessed December 21, 2020, www.glaad.org.
17. Bree Fram, personal communication, October 27, 2019.
18. Bree Fram, personal communication, November 11, 2019.
19. Matt Thompson, "How to Spark Panic and Confusion in Three Tweets," *Atlantic*, January 13, 2019, www.theatlantic.com.
20. Dominic Holden, "Gen. Mattis Says He Has No Plans to Repeal LGBT Military Service," BuzzFeed News, January 12, 2017, www.buzzfeednews.com.
21. Michelle Mark, "Trump May Have Announced the Transgender Military Ban to Save a Bill Funding the Border Wall," *Business Insider*, July 26, 2017, www.businessinsider.com.
22. Bree Fram, personal communication, October 27, 2019.
23. Bree Fram, personal communication, November 9, 2019.
24. Bree Fram, personal communication, November 11, 2019.
25. Bree Fram, author's personal recollection and personal records.
26. Ibid.
27. The four cases are *Doe v. Trump* (8/9/2017), *Karnoski v. Trump* (8/28/2017), *Stone v. Trump* (8/28/2017), and *Stockman v. Trump* (9/5/2017).
28. *Donald J. Trump, President of the United States, et al., Petitioners v. Jane Doe 2, et al.* Petition for a Writ of Certiorari before Judgment, page 92a, accessed February 29, 2020, www.justice.gov.
29. SPARTA, "Official Statement: We Are Disappointed in Today's Ruling," Twitter, January 22, 2019, https://twitter.com/sparta_pride/status/1087749980847308800.
30. Bree Fram, personal communication, October 27, 2019.

31. Tom Vanden Brook, "Democrats Blast Trump Policy That Bans Most Transgender Troops from Serving," *USA Today*, February 27, 2019, www.usatoday.com.
32. Congressman Anthony Brown, "In the News," February 28, 2019, accessed February 29, 2020, https://anthonybrown.house.gov.
33. Zack Ford, "Trump Administration Tells Congress That Being Transgender Is Like Having a Disease," ThinkProgress, February 28, 2019, accessed February 29, 2020, https://thinkprogress.org.
34. Ibid.
35. Dave Philipps, "Transgender Troops Caught between a Welcoming Military and a Hostile Government," *New York Times*, March 9, 2019, www.nytimes.com.
36. "Directive-Type Memorandum (DTM)-19-004—Military Service by Transgender Persons and Persons with Gender Dysphoria," Office of the Deputy Secretary of Defense, March 12, 2019, accessed February 29, 2020, www.esd.whs.mil.
37. Barbara Starr and Caroline Kelly, "US Navy Grants First Waiver for Transgender Service Member to Serve under Their Preferred Gender," CNN.com, May 15, 2020, www.cnn.com.
38. Seline San Felice, "Meet the Fort Meade Trans Women Fighting the Transgender Military Ban," *Capital Gazette*, April 24, 2019, www.capitalgazette.com.

Chapter 6. Serving in the Future

1. Samantha Allen, "Meet Map Pesqueira, the First Trans Person Prevented from Joining the Military by Trump's Ban," *Daily Beast*, April 19, 2019, www.thedailybeast.com.
2. "Chairman Smith Statement on DoD Implementation of the Ban on Transgender Military Service," House Armed Services Committee, March 12, 2019, https://armedservices.house.gov.
3. Bree Fram, personal communication, January 26, 2020.
4. Ibid.
5. Ibid.
6. Ibid.
7. Bree Fram, personal communication, February 4, 2020.
8. Ibid.
9. Ibid.
10. Bree Fram, personal communication, February 7, 2020.
11. Ibid.
12. "Airman" is the term used by the U.S. Air Force regardless of the sex/gender of the service member.
13. Bree Fram, personal communication, January 31, 2020.
14. Ibid.
15. "Morning Consult National Tracking Poll #170711, July 27–29, 2017, Crosstabulations," https://morningconsult.com.

16. "In U.S., 71% Support Transgender People Serving in Military," Gallup, June 20, 2019, https://news.gallup.com.
17. S. L. Dunlap, I. W. Holloway, C. E. Pickering, et al., "Support for Transgender Military Service from Active Duty United States Military Personnel," *Sex Res Soc Policy* (2020), https://doi.org/10.1007/s13178-020-00437-x.
18. "Military Chiefs of Staff Unanimous: Transgender Inclusion Has Not Harmed Unit Cohesion," Palm Center, April 25, 2018, www.palmcenter.org.
19. Donald C. Arthur, USN, (Ret.), Gale Pollock, USA (Ret.), Alan M. Steinman, USCG (Ret.), Nathaniel Frank, Diane H. Mazur, and Aaron Belkin, "DoD's Transgender Ban Has Harmed Military Readiness," Palm Center, November 2020, www.palmcenter.org.
20. Rebecca Kheel, "Biden Under Pressure to Remove Trump Transgender Military Ban Quickly," *Hill*, November 27, 2020, https://thehill.com.
21. "New Research on Military's Transgender Ban Lends Urgency to Biden's Pledge to End It on Day One," Palm Center, December 28, 2020, www.palmcenter.org. See also Rear Admiral (Ret.) Alan M. Steinman's report, "Blueprint for Immediate Restoration of Inclusive Transgender Military Policy," Palm Center, July 26, 2020, updated November 8, 2020, www.palmcenter.org.
22. "Executive Order 14004 of January 25, 2021, Executive Order on Enabling All Qualified Americans to Serve Their Country in Uniform," *Code of Federal Regulations*, title 3 (2021): 7471–7473, www.federalregister.gov.
23. Ibid.
24. Ailsa Chang, "Biden Ends Ban on Trans People Serving Openly in the Military," *All Things Considered*, National Public Radio (NPR), January 25, 2021, www.npr.org.

ABOUT THE CONTRIBUTORS

Zaneford Alvarez has served in the U.S. Army as a behavioral health technician for seven years. He has worked with patients experiencing anxiety, depression, PTSD, and substance abuse. Zane is currently stationed in Germany and works with NATO allies and partners, focusing on the medical presence in Europe, Africa, and the Middle East.

Tyler "Billy" Billiet enlisted in the U.S. Air Force in 2013 as a geospatial intelligence analyst and intends to make a career of military service. The Air Force has brought him to Beale AFB in Northern California. Beale is his first, and so far only, duty station. He says, "I love it!" and writes that Northern California is a giant playground for all of his outdoor hobbies such as snowboarding, camping, and hiking.

A. Jordan Blisk served as a senior airman in the United States Air Force Reserves from 2011 to 2015. Jordan earned his Juris Doctor from the University of Colorado Law School, where he became the first openly transgender graduate. As a lawyer, he uses his skills to serve the transgender and veteran communities. Jordan resides in Denver, where he enjoys fly fishing and camping with his two dogs, Hamilton and Huxley.

Rachael Evelyn Booth struggled with being transgender from the age of five. She joined the U.S. Navy during Vietnam and served for nine years as a linguist, married twice, and had children in an attempt to try to find her place in society. In 1991, she tried to commit suicide and decided she'd suffered enough. Rachael is a retired computer scientist, a guitarist/singer, and an author of two books, one of which is a memoir of her life.

Sabrina Bruce served seven years in the U.S. Air Force and has recently joined the U.S. Space Force, where she will be working on cyber defense. She transitioned in 2017 and regards that decision as the best she has ever made. Sabrina is currently stationed in the United Kingdom and enjoys sightseeing with her partner.

Danielle "Dani" Butler served twenty-two years in the U.S. Marine Corps as a meteorologist, instructor, and recruiter, retiring in 1998 as a master sergeant. Since retirement, she has worked as a contractor with the U.S. Army. Dani transitioned in 2018 and now loves her life. When not working, she plays her bagpipes, rides her bicycle with a cycling club, and rides her motorcycle with the local American Legion. She also supports others through her leadership with the Rappahannock Region Transgender Group. In 2021, Dani and her wife will celebrate forty-two years of marriage. Together they have four children, thirteen grandchildren, and a great-granddaughter on the way.

Allison Caputo holds the rank of captain and is the chief of planning at Joint Task Force West in San Antonio, Texas. She is a 1995 graduate of the U.S. Coast Guard Academy and holds a master's degree in Marine affairs from the University of Rhode Island. A previous commanding officer of the USCGC *Campbell* (WMEC 909), she has more than eleven years of sea duty on both coasts.

Sterling J. Crutcher joined the U.S. Air Force in 2015. After basic training, he was stationed at Barksdale AFB. Sterling started his transition from female to male in February 2016 and has received nothing but support from his commander. Sterling says that they have recognized his hard work and dedication to his path and that he has earned their respect. This has allowed him the opportunity to educate others regarding trans military service.

Blake Dremann, lieutenant commander, is a Navy Supply Corps officer with fifteen years of service and eleven deployments. He has been on the front lines of several integrations to include the repeal of DADT, women on submarines, and repeal of the trans ban. He has several personal commendations and was the recipient of the Navy's highest logistics award in 2015 and the DoD Pride Military Leadership Award in 2018.

Tucker Duval is currently a second year MBA candidate at the University of Georgia. He is thoroughly enjoying nesting in Athens with his partner, Sarah, and their two dogs and one cat. He served in the U.S. Army for five years as an engineer officer. Tucker graduated from West Point in 2012.

Eve is a sixteen-year sailor and seasoned member of the intelligence community. She has deployed numerous times on three different surface vessels in support of Operation Enduring Freedom, counterproliferation missions, and multiple joint nation partnership exercises. She has served two tours providing real-time support to units conducting special operations, and two as a tactical information warfare instructor. She currently serves as a nuclear reactor refueling/overhaul project coordinator and maintenance safety manager in Newport News, Virginia.

Jamie Hash enlisted in the U.S. Air Force in 2011 and currently serves as a manpower analyst. She began her career as an aircraft armament technician and, after deploying to Southwest Asia in 2014–2015 in the joint coalition against ISIS, retrained into manpower. Outside of the military, she has completed an MS in organizational performance improvement and is pursuing a graduate certificate in data analytics from the Air Force Institute of Technology.

Nate Hoang is a captain in the U.S. Army. He is very much in love with his profession as a general dentist and considers it a great privilege to serve as one. Nate recognizes that his experience as a Korean American trans man, who happens to be in the Army, is unique and hopes that his contribution illuminates one perspective of being transgender in the military.

Alexandria Holder is an Arabic linguist with over sixteen years of experience. Currently serving in the U.S. Air Force, she has spent the bulk of her service at Fort Meade, Maryland, though she has deployed twice, once to Afghanistan. She currently lives in Monterey, California, with her wife of ten years and her four children.

Miranda Jones, a lieutenant colonel, now retired, joined the U.S. Marine Corps in early 1989 and has served in combat, with tours to Iraq and Afghanistan. She is married with four children, all of whom are aware and supportive of her gender fluidity. Miranda says that she is still very much figuring out where she is on the spectrum of gender identity and how she can best live her life while balancing her male and female qualities.

Kris Moore is a lieutenant, surface warfare officer, in the U.S. Navy. He enlisted in the Navy in 2005 and was later accepted to the U.S. Naval Academy (USNA) class of 2014. LT Moore was stationed on a guided missile destroyer (DDG) homeported out of Norfolk, VA, from 2014 to 2018 and deployed once to the 5th and 6th Fleet areas of operation. He served as a company officer at USNA from 2018 to 2021, where he earned a master's in leadership, education, and development from George Washington University.

Caroline A. Morrison has served as a religious affairs specialist in the U.S. Army for over sixteen years. She is a wife, mama of four amazing Army brats, a veteran of both Operation Iraqi Freedom and Operation Enduring Freedom, a proud woman, and an American soldier.

Sebastian Nemec is a public affairs non-commissioned officer in the Minnesota National Guard. He has been serving since 2011 and deployed once to Kuwait in 2014–2015. He has earned a BA in cultural entrepreneurship with a minor in journalism from the University of Minnesota, Duluth, and is working toward an MBA. He is passionate about helping tell the stories of LGBTQ+ people.

Molly T. Sackman is a petty officer first class in the U.S. Navy. She enlisted when she was twenty to escape the mediocrity of working at Petco and to get out of Tulsa, Oklahoma. She has served as an AEGIS fire controlman. She has conducted six deployments, visiting thirteen countries including Vietnam, Thailand, Dubai, and South Korea, and has provided transgender training for her ship. When home, she enjoys spending time with her loving wife, Crystal, and riding and wrenching on her motorcycles.

Natalie Seidel was born in Germany but raised in Ohio and serves as a petty officer second class in the U.S. Navy. Married to Samantha Seidel, she has enjoyed many adventures, living in places from Paris to Honolulu. Natalie brought her skills as a junior high social studies teacher and Fulbright scholar to the U.S. Navy. She has advocated on issues related to trans service, including in a public forum with her commanding officer and has been accepted into the National Intelligence University's Master of Science in Strategic Intelligence program.

Seth Stang is a staff sergeant in the U.S. Air Force and a photojournalist/public affairs specialist. He has been stationed at Minot Air Force Base in support of bomber and missile missions; the Uniformed Services University, where he helped lead a Navy Security Forces Team; and Wright-Patterson Air Force Base, where he was the NCOIC of Open Skies and served as a U.S. diplomat. He now serves as the NCOIC of social media for the U.S. Air Force Academy. He has also given birth to two children with his wife, a transgender Air Force Security Forces veteran.

Sheri A. Swokowski served 35 years in the U.S. Army National Guard, retiring with the rank of colonel. She also holds a PhD in leadership. A career infantry soldier, she led a light infantry unit, deployed twice, and served at battalion, brigade, and department levels. While prohibited from serving authentically in uniform, she did so, post-retirement, as a Pentagon senior analyst. An internationally known advocate for transgender rights and military service, she has been featured on CNN, MSNBC, Headline News, and Al-Jazeera.

Hanna Tripp served in the U.S. Air Force from 2009 to 2013. As an aerial gunner, she deployed to Iraq, where she flew twenty combat sorties in support of special operation forces and was awarded an Air Medal for her actions. She was a community service fellow with The Mission Continues at the Office of Congressman Joseph P. Kennedy III. Hanna is currently a district aide and veterans caseworker for U.S. Representative Seth Moulton (D-MA).

Mak Vaden has been in the U.S. Army for thirteen years, serving as a 35F intelligence analyst and 35M human intelligence collector. Currently a staff sergeant serving full-time with the Georgia Army National Guard, he also served at Fort Hood, Texas, and deployed to Iraq from 2008 to 2009 and the Southwest Border mission in 2011. He has had the honor of being recognized as distinguished honor graduate from the Senior Leaders Course.

Evan Young retired from the U.S. Army with the rank of major. A native of Little Rock, Arkansas, he is a graduate of Northwestern State University of Louisiana with a bachelor's degree in English. He also earned a master's degree in management information systems from Nova Southeastern University. Young is the former president of the Transgender American Veterans Association (TAVA) and former president of the board of directors for the Arkansas Transgender Equality Coalition (ArTEC).

ABOUT THE EDITORS

Máel Embser-Herbert is Professor of Sociology at Hamline University. They are a veteran of the U.S. Army and author of *Camouflage Isn't Only for Combat: Gender, Sexuality, and Women in the Military* (1998, NYU Press) and *The U.S. Military's "Don't Ask, Don't Tell" Policy: A Reference Handbook* (2007, Praeger Security International).

Bree Fram is a lieutenant colonel in the U.S. Space Force who has held command at the squadron level, led USAF security cooperation with Iraq, and led space acquisition programs. She is married with two children and holds graduate degrees in astronautical engineering and national security and strategic studies.

LGBTQ POLITICS SERIES

General Editors: Susan Burgess and Heath Fogg Davis

Disrupting Dignity: Rethinking Power and Progress in LGBTQ Lives
Stephen M. Engel and Timothy S. Lyle

With Honor and Integrity: Transgender Troops in Their Own Words
Edited by Máel Embser-Herbert and Bree Fram